FINDING
FREEDOM
FROM THE
SHAME
OF THE
PAST

Mike Fehlauer

D1304876

CREATION
HOUSE

FINDING FREEDOM FROM THE SHAME OF THE PAST
by Mike Fehlauer
Published by Creation House
A division of Strang Communications Company
600 Rinehart Road
Lake Mary, Florida 32746
www.creationhouse.com
www.charismalife.com

Unless otherwise noted, all Scripture quotations are
from the New King James Version of the Bible.
Copyright © 1979, 1980, 1982 by Thomas Nelson, Inc.,
publishers. Used by permission.

Scripture quotations marked KJV are from the
King James Version of the Bible.

Scripture quotations marked AMP are from the Amplified
Bible. Old Testament Copyright © 1965, 1987 by the
Zondervan Corporation. The Amplified New Testament
Copyright © 1954, 1958, 1987 by the Lockman Foundation.
Used by permission.

Scripture quotations marked NAS are from the New
American Standard Bible. Copyright © 1960, 1962, 1963, 1968,
1971, 1972, 1973, 1975, 1977 by the Lockman Foundation.
Used by permission.

Library of Congress Cataloging-in-Publication Data:
Fehlauer, Mike
Finding freedom from the shame of the past / Mike Fehlauer
        p. cm
    ISBN 0-88419-583-X
    1. Christian life. 2. Fehlauer, Mike   I Title
BV4501.2.F42 1999
248.4—DC21   98-31375
                                                                                    CIP

9 0 1 2 3 4 5 6 BBG 8 7 6 5 4 3 2
Printed in the United States of America

This book is dedicated...

To my heavenly Father—when You saw this prodigal poke his head over the horizon, You met me while I was "still a far way off."

To my beautiful and faithful wife, Bonnie—Honey, you are an awesome partner and woman of God. God has used you to change my life. I love you.

To my two children, Janae and Josiah—you may not realize how much joy you both bring me. I am proud of you both. Your hunger for God has challenged me on more than one occasion. I have learned from both of you.

To my family—Mom and Dad, you have been great supporters. Doug and Toni, you have given me great encouragement and faith. You all are the best.

—Acknowledgments—

Robb and Linda Thompson—thank you for being there and providing an environment of love, acceptance, and forgiveness. Robb, thank you for believing in me, even when I didn't believe in myself, and for preaching the message of God's grace in such an uncompromising fashion.

The men who worked with me at East Coast Christian Center—heaven has recorded your acts of kindness, mercy, and wisdom. Dave, you are truly an example of faithfulness and stability. Ray, your love covered and protected me at your own expense, demonstrating your character and friendship. Eric, you could have quit, but you chose to stay. Dan, you have been a powerful instrument of restoration.

Andrew and Jamie Wommack—thanks for being such great cheerleaders as Bonnie and I began a new season of life and ministry. You have challenged me to a life of simplicity, integrity, and sincerity.

Our partners who support Foundation Ministries with prayers and finances—thank you for recognizing the lives that together we are changing.

Pastor Ted Haggard and New Life Church—it is an honor to be a part of this wonderful congregation. It has changed our lives. Thank you, Ted, that when Tom Freiling asked whom you thought Creation House should publish, you said me! Thank you for creating a greater hunger for prayer and for expanding our vision. We are glad you are our pastor.

Steve and Joy Strang and Tom Freiling—thank you for believing in me and this message. I also thank the Creation House staff for helping to put this project together.

Dave Roberson—thank you for showing me how to release my Teacher to teach me and for opening up the Scriptures in such a powerful way.

Contents

Foreword

S I WAS PREPARING TO LEAVE MY office and drive to Praise Mountain for three days of prayer and fasting with my sixteen-year-old daughter, Christy, I glanced out of my office window and saw her standing patiently beside my car waiting for me. Watching her carefully, my heart was moved deeply as my love and appreciation for her surged to the surface of my emotions. I knew she was a gift. I knew she was special. I also knew that I could give her a strong foundation for life by simply living well, or I could foolishly inflict her with shame, hurt, and lifelong instability by making poor decisions. In that moment, I knew I never wanted to do or say anything that would hurt her or to allow anyone else ever to hurt her. The fact that she is worth living and dying for was highlighted in my heart and mind.

Every Christian I know is familiar with these emotions. I have watched people experience the same sentiment: a grateful pastor admiring his congregation; a mother moved by her daughter's piano recital; a young dad proud of his son's performance on the pitcher's mound; an elderly couple warmly glancing at one another. It's these emotions that Mike Fehlauer is drawing us back to in this book. He's encouraging us to grow in life with Christ and to manifest grace and dignity. He's teaching us how to deal with life's most difficult moments. When we're all tempted to be selfish, Mike teaches to do the right thing—the right thing for God and for the dignity of those who love us most.

Looking back on the day I saw Christy from my office, I know I was realizing that, through my daughter, God has placed a constraint on my life and has given me a wonderful motivation to live well. I know that I must be extra careful to live a life that is worthy of someone else's admiration and love. Because of the responsibility I have to guard her innocence, it would be foolish and shortsighted to have a lifestyle that is anything less than pure and godly.

I believe this is one reason why God teaches us to have healthy relationships. Our spouses, friends, family members, and other relationships within the body of Christ are external constraints that motivate us to develop the internal constraints necessary to live a life of integrity, a life that is the same in private as it is in public.

At one time or another, the enemy or the world will tempt us to fail by saying to us, "Go ahead; no one will find out." Or, "Just do it this once." It's in those moments that we have a major decision to make. When we make the correct decision, we experience a great sense of victory. But when we make the wrong decision, we have to know how to stand up again, building external support and constructing internal dignity in the hope that, with Christ, our lives can, and will, get better.

Too often, though, the appeal of sin lingers. When Satan tempted Eve, he was successful because he was crafty enough to make Eve believe her life would be better if she disobeyed God. Unfortunately, the consequences of sin are always much more tragic than we expect. What begins with a simple entertained thought turns easily into a lifestyle of deception and shame. Like the old adage says:

> Sin will take you further than you want to go,
> Cost you more than you want to pay,
> And keep you longer than you want to stay.

The good news, of course, is that the power of God is much greater than the power of sin. In 1 John 1:7, the Bible offers a three-step progression toward exercising freedom from sin: "If we walk in the light as He is in the light, we have fellowship with one another, and the blood of Jesus Christ His Son cleanses us from all sin."

First of all, our lives must be "in the light." This means that we are entirely honest before God and people. We should all keep a mentality of complete openness about our lives. Every Christian needs a friend to whom they can tell anything, for when we lay our lives bare, concealing nothing, there is no possibility of falling into secret sin and deception.

Naturally, when our lives are uncovered, we can have genuine fellowship with other believers. The innocence that is produced through walking in the light enables us to connect with people, creating a fraternity of Christians empowered to encourage and admonish one another on toward godly lives. Then, when we are both in the light and experiencing true fellowship, the blood of Jesus can begin to flow into our hearts, purifying us from all sin and leading us toward true repentance so that we can turn away from sin once and for all.

Until this progression is successfully established in our lives, we will continue to struggle with temptation and sin. That reality begs these questions: What do we do when we fail? How do we get back into God's perfect plan for our lives? How do we respond to His grace instead of responding to guilt and frustration?

It is this dilemma that Mike Fehlauer so adequately addresses in the following book. An honorable man of God with a refined, distinctive understanding of the unmerited favor of God, Mike offers a practical view of a lifestyle of grace. As Mike's pastor, I know that he has tasted the bitter fruit of shame; more importantly, as this book shows, Mike has tasted the wonderful fruit of God's extraordinary kindness and love. With every page, Mike's thoughts on freedom and grace resonate from a deeply personal understanding of Christ's work on the cross.

If you are hurting, this book is for you. If you are full of shame and grief, this book is for you. If you refuse to believe that a holy God can forgive someone such as you, this book is for you. Read it with the understanding that you have been invited to peer deeply into the eyes of Jesus and realize that He loves you without condition. Read it knowing that He wants to embrace you, to change you, and to call you His own. Read it, and let your life be renewed as you dwell in the wonderful presence of His love.

—Ted Haggard
Pastor, New Life Church
Colorado Springs, CO

Out of My Own
Personal Darkness

T'S AMAZING, THE TERRIFYING THOUGHTS THAT run through your mind when you're holding a gun to your head. *If I pull the trigger, will anybody hear the sound? How long will it be before anyone finds the body? My hand is shaking...will I hit the target?*

In my case, I was the most unlikely person in the world to be sitting there in the darkness of my car with a .357 magnum trembling in my hand and aimed squarely at my head. After all, I was the pastor of a successful, growing, central Florida church. I had a wonderful family—a beautiful wife and two lovely children.

So, what was I doing sitting on the side of the road with the cold steel of a gun barrel pressed against my skull?

Looking through the foggy windshield at my church building across the street, I thought long and hard about the circumstances that led to that confused moment. That very night I had scheduled a guest speaker to preach, and I was supposed to introduce him! But, as I watched members of my congregation file into the building, I sat glued to my car seat, filled with terror and unable to move.

Four years earlier, my wife and I had arrived in the city, driving a rented U-Haul truck, with great expectations for building a church. Life couldn't have been better. We were young, in love, and the idea of the new pastorate filled every moment with an unusual thrill. After checking into a motel, we immediately began looking for a house to rent; within a few hours, we experienced success. It was on the main boulevard of this central Florida city, and although it was priced right and convenient, it came with the requisite problems of a main street—noise, traffic, and, worst of all, beer bottles and other trash liberally tossed onto the lawn. But that was of little concern—we had more important challenges ahead.

I began pastoring the new church, and with the multitude of responsibilities associated with a new position of leadership, our lives were filled with a fresh excitement. We hardly had time for work around the house, but grudgingly, I soon decided that I needed to stay on top of the growing trash heap that was accumulating outside in the front yard.

It was a Saturday morning when I first confronted the trash problem, the obvious result of a raucous beachfront Friday night. I was out on the front lawn picking up the beer bottles when I noticed a paperback book by the roadside. Out of curiosity I picked it up and started leafing through the pages. It didn't take long to realize it was pornographic—no dirty pictures, but a collection of pornographic stories that immediately carved crystal clear sexual images in my mind. I tossed out the book, not realizing the mental replicas couldn't be forgotten quite so easily.

After a week or two those images began coming back to my mind with a vengeance. Looking back, I am reminded of how a photographic image grows more and more in focus as it is developed. These pictures built a stronger and stronger foothold in my subconscious, and I began waking up in the middle of the night thinking about them. As the months passed, they became the first thing I thought about when I awoke in the morning and the last thing I pictured before I went to sleep at night.

Being a young pastor, I struggled to deny the thoughts. I read the Bible and prayed. But, having no experience in fighting pornography or sexual sin, I had little knowledge of how to deal with the problem other than with sheer willpower—*which I discovered was a futile weapon in the face of such an enemy.*

The battlefield was slanted against me as well. Because of the unique nature of this county's obscenity laws, there is an amazing range of obscene and pornographic services offered throughout the county. Within a short drive from my home there were strip joints, massage parlors, escort services, bars, adult bookstores, X-rated movies, and more. Therefore, even my daily drive through the city exposed me to a barrage of signs and advertisements that kept those desires in the forefront of my mind.

It wasn't long before I ventured into the world of pornographic magazines and videos. During my lunch hour…while my wife, Bonnie, was away from home…any private moment I could get, I spent looking at magazines and videos. After each time, I became overwhelmed with feelings of shame. Under the weight of guilt I would promise myself and God that I would never again give in to those dark, all too familiar passions. Yet after the emotion of guilt would fade, I would find myself visiting the places I'd swore I'd never go to again.

The fascination progressed until I had to experience more than a simple magazine or video could provide.

THAT'S WHEN I FIRST VISITED A MASSAGE PARLOR.

Terrified at first, I made two or three initial visits just to ask about prices, appointments…anything I could think of as an excuse just to go take a look at the place. After several weeks of this activity, I finally made an appointment for a sexual encounter under the guise of a massage. I remember my nervousness as the "hostess" escorted me through a maze of hallways. I also remember my nervousness as I entered one of the dimly lit rooms. I immediately noticed the masseuse's table in the center of the room. I would later discover this was only to give an appearance of credibility. Beneath the table was a shelf that contained a number of neatly stacked towels and a display of numerous oils and lotions. Once alone, part of me wanted to run, yet lust and curiosity kept me standing there…waiting.

In a few moments, a different, younger-looking girl entered the room wearing a short skirt, stockings, and heels. She reached one hand behind her, shutting the door. Even from a distance I was overwhelmed with the smell of cheap perfume. She began to undress as she moved toward me....

I'll never forget the sick feeling, the guilt, and the terror I experienced once it was over. The urge to run that I had before came back now with the force of a hurricane. I rushed out of the building, avoiding the gaze of the next customers, hoping that none of them would recognize me. Instead of the sexual "rush" that I had hoped for and that the sex industry seemed to promise, all I could feel was disgust and self-loathing. Driving home, I remember that I began to scream. I continued to scream through tears of anguish until I pulled into our driveway. I slowly walked into my house, hoarse and ashamed.

That first experience opened a gateway to a flood of sin. I heard an evangelist say once, "Our lives always go in the direction of our most dominant thought." That was certainly true in my case.

Strangely enough, during this time I still kept up my pastoral duties. I still preached sermons, visited the sick, and managed church affairs. Absolutely no one had any idea of my double life. I soon realized I was bound—addicted—to these episodes of illicit sexual expression. I discovered that a sexual addiction was unlike an addiction to drugs—it left no telltale signs! There were no needle marks, no physical changes, no lethargy, and no signs of weakness. I was keeping my double life going full tilt, and it left no incriminating trail whatsoever.

Today, I realize that this sheer invisibility of sexual addiction is one of Satan's greatest weapons in the battle. A double life of sexual sin leaves an obscure trail, therefore there is very little chance of being caught or even noticed. It's fairly easy to spot someone in the advanced stages of heroin or crack addiction—but much more difficult in the case of sexual sin.

Killer Ted Bundy, on Florida's death row, confessed that he was able to compartmentalize his crimes in his mind so that after brutally murdering a woman, he could clean himself up, go to work, and act completely normal. As horrible as it is to compare yourself with someone as overtly evil as Ted Bundy, I understand that ability to compartmentalize your thoughts into distinctly separate areas of your mind. One moment I could be in my office counseling a church member, and within an hour I would be sitting in a dark, smoke-filled strip joint.

I thought about that double life while sitting in my car across the street from the church. I begged God to kill me, or at least make me invisible so I could disappear from my family, my friends, and my loved ones.

THEN, I ALSO REMEMBERED MY GROWING PARANOIA.

My escapades seemed to take place in three-month cycles. For three months I would experience relief and life free as a pastor, family man, and friend. But then Satan always knew the right buttons to push. It might have been a television program, a magazine ad, or a comment on the radio, but whatever it was, I would find myself once again inside an adult bookstore, in a massage parlor, or calling an escort service.

I was finding it harder and harder to cover my tracks as my church continued to grow. I became fearful that sooner or later someone would see me in the "wrong part of town" or perhaps walking into an X-rated movie. I began to wear complex disguises and took more care to use back doors and alleys.

THE PARANOIA CONTINUED TO GROW...

It began dominating church affairs. I began to argue with friends whom I deeply loved, and I became despotic in church meetings. My wife literally cried a river of tears trying to uncover the source of my hurt and pain, not knowing the horrible reality that flowed underneath my raging personality—gushing forth like a river of molten lava.

Tragically and predictably, that egotistical attitude began to systematically cut me off from the very ones that could have helped me. I continued to estrange myself from even my closest friends. The pressure became too great; that's when it seemed that the only real end to my pain would come through the pistol I held in my hand.

While sitting there in the darkened car, images of the past flooded through my mind. The hiding, the disguises, the shame, the disappointment—all came rushing forward like a raging army of darkness. Somehow, by the grace of God, I was so afraid of dying that I didn't have the courage to pull the trigger. Still shaking, I uncocked the pistol, quietly laid the gun down on the car seat, and slowly drove home through blinding tears.

The implosion caused by my reckless and sinful behavior had finally caused my life to collapse around me. I felt as if I were suffocating—alone and without hope.

That night I finally confessed *everything* to my

7

wife, Bonnie. Holding nothing back, I told her the nightmarish history from the moment I picked up that paperback book on the front lawn to the moment I dropped the gun on the seat of the car.

Of course, she was devastated. I fully expected her to leave, slam the door in my face, and never return. But I hadn't counted on the depth of Bonnie's commitment to God and His unlimited grace in the face of a horrific circumstance. I did know that the healing and recovery might take years. I started sleeping on the couch, knowing that although there was forgiveness at the cross, the consequences of my sin would take great time and even greater effort to repair.

Although it was the most difficult time of my life, over the next few years God would begin to work a miracle in my life and in the life of my family. Along with my wife's determination not to give up, God graciously helped us break the bondage of that horrible stronghold and begin a new life together.

BUT IT WASN'T GOING TO BE SIMPLE OR EASY.

Perhaps the greatest lesson I have learned as a result of God's work of restoration is that a *stronghold* is *any* system of destructive thinking. In my case, I had fought a stronghold of sexual thoughts, ideas, and desires. In other cases, a stronghold may be an intense struggle with drugs, alcohol, violence, power, self-image, finances, or any other addictive thinking that preoccupies your mind *to the point of being obsessive*. Therefore, while Christ offers complete forgiveness and salvation, we must still break the mental stronghold that often has taken years, and occasionally a lifetime, to build.

As a result of the decisions I had made, the greatest stronghold that I faced was the stronghold of the past. I knew the husband I needed to be. I knew the father I wanted to be. I was very aware of the man of God I desired to be. But that man seemed a million miles away. There was a time in my life where I couldn't see any way to escape the strangling tentacles of the past. But then, Jesus graciously began to teach me life-giving principles about His love and grace.

The principles that I will share in this book have the ability to release the dynamic of God's grace and bring restoration and freedom from the shame of the past in your life. These principles also have the ability to establish a heritage of righteousness for your life and family. My hope is that you will learn at my expense. If you will apply these truths, they will help you to build a solid foundation for your life and family and will

JESUS' LOVE AND GRACE HELPED ME ESCAPE THE STRANGLING TENTACLES OF THE PAST.

establish the character and faith needed to finish strong the course of your life with Christ. By walking through these steps, God by His grace empowered me to find freedom from the shame of the past!

9

God's Answer to Shame

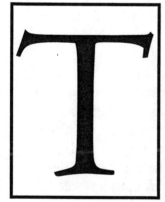HE PERIODIC SWELLS OF WATER underneath the boat cause it to rock gently back and forth. The rhythmic motion of the lake produces an almost hypnotic state, carrying Peter's thoughts back to that fateful night. Squeezing his eyes tightly shut he winces painfully as the memory floods his imagination. Jesus had warned them that things would change suddenly. The disciples finally figured out that He was talking about His death. Still, Peter was unable, like the rest, to accept this fact. In a heated moment Peter declared loudly that he would die with Jesus if that's what it would come to. "I meant it. I meant it with all of my heart," Peter

whispers under his breath. He remembers that everyone had scattered in fear as Jesus was arrested. He also remembers that he had followed from a distance. The air that night was cool, and the fire burning nearby had looked safe enough. Standing near the warmth of the blaze, the glow from the flickering flames threw shadows across Peter's face. Even in the darkness, a woman standing nearby was able to recognize him as one of the Nazarene's disciples.

As he sits in his boat, Peter can still hear himself swearing to the woman that he knew nothing about this man from Galilee. The most crushing part of that whole night, though, was the look that Jesus gave Peter right after his third denial. As they were leading Jesus through the outer court, their eyes met. That's when something broke in Peter. His face flushed, he couldn't hold back the hot tears that coursed through the lines of his weathered face.

After that night Peter figured he was finished. He was sure that he would forever be known as the coward who turned his back on the Teacher. He couldn't even imagine being forgiven, let alone carrying on the work that he began with the Messiah. It was over, he concluded. He had failed. It could never be right again. *He* could never be right again. Surrendering to the silent enemy of anguish and despair, Peter decided to go back to what he was doing when he first met this miracle man—fishing. *The shame of failure can run deep.*

Suddenly, Peter feels a hand on his shoulder, bringing his thoughts back to the present. He turns his head and is reminded that he is not alone. With him in his boat of hopelessness are James and John.

HOPELESSNESS: A FRUIT OF SHAME

Peter had been crushed with the feeling of hopelessness. *Hopelessness* is a fruit of shame. I believe that hopelessness is the ultimate goal of temptation; I don't believe that Satan's primary goal when tempting us with evil is to get us to commit acts of sin. Please don't misunderstand me—Satan's desire is to get us to commit sin. But this is not his ultimate goal. Satan's primary purpose is that *if* or *when* we give in to his temptations, he then can come to us with a sense of hopelessness. Such hopelessness strips us of any expectation of ever being able to be freed from his demonic control over our minds and the dictates of our flesh.

What happened with Peter is a perfect example of this method of self-destruction. As we look at Peter's life, we can see the cancerous process of hopelessness.

Right after Peter, for the third time, vehemently denied that he knew Jesus, Luke 22:62 records these seven words: "So Peter went out and wept bitterly." Within these seven words we can hear the fierce pain and despair of a man who had failed God. After his denial came shame and disgust over his cowardice. Then his shame gave birth to hopelessness, which results in three self-destructive attitudes.

HOPELESSNESS RESULTS
IN RESIGNATION.

Once hopelessness set in, Peter then resigned himself to his failure. He abandoned himself to defeat. Hopelessness will cause us to lose all sight of the ability to conquer our passions. Proverbs

13:12 says, "Hope deferred makes the heart sick, but when the desire comes, it is a tree of life."

Each time hopelessness sets in, every other failure of the past will come back to our minds like a torrent. We begin to calculate the affect of every defeat, resulting in the conclusion that we will never win over our weaknesses. "What's the use," we say. "I've always been a slave to my desires, and it appears that I always will be."

This is exactly what Satan wants you and I to think. Satan wants us to surrender ourselves to his destructive leading. The problem is, once we embrace this attitude, we will never escape the shame of the past. Nor will we discover the confidence and strength we need to resist the temptations of today. We will find ourselves in a cycle of defeat that will leave us forever crushed and in despair.

HOPELESSNESS EXALTS OUR SIN OVER THE CROSS.

Hopelessness allows the past to have the final word. Whether the past represents something we have done or something that has been done to us, hopelessness gives the past a higher place of honor than the finished work of Christ. Hopelessness accepts the natural (our sin or failure) over the supernatural (Christ's sacrifice on the cross). When we lose hope, we begin to place more value on our actions and the actions of others than we do on Jesus' ultimate act of love.

By doing so, whether we realize it or not, we are dishonoring the cross. We are placing more faith on what has happened in our lives than upon what happened two thousand years ago at Calvary. This is the ultimate example of pride. *Pride* is simply lifting up our opinion and feelings above the truth of the Scriptures. The Scriptures declare that we are forgiven. The Word of God declares that the blood of Jesus cleanses us from all sin.

> If we confess our sins, He is faithful and just to forgive us our sins and to cleanse us from all unrighteousness.
>
> —1 JOHN 1:9

His holy Word says that regardless of what anyone has done to us, we are His glory, His prized possession, His ultimate satisfaction.

HOPELESSNESS STEALS YOUR PURPOSE.

The third thing that hopelessness does is steal our sense of purpose. Once we lose hope, we lose vision. Our destiny becomes clouded by the events of the past. Our eyes are darkened, and we become blind to our future. We turn a deaf ear to the encouraging words of our friends. Our senses are shadowed by our distorted reasonings and perceptions. The encouraging words we read in Scripture mean little, if anything, to us.

Even the apostle Peter initially refused to accept the encouragement of Jesus Himself. Jesus prophesied that Peter would deny Him. But He also tried to encourage Peter, saying that after being restored, he would be a vessel used to strengthen others. After Jesus' Resurrection, the angel at the tomb instructed Mary to tell the disciples—*including Peter*—of His Resurrection (Mark 16:7). Jesus wanted to make sure that Peter knew that he was still included in the gospel mission.

The Book of Luke indicates that when the apostles received Mary's words of Jesus' Resurrection, the others "did not believe them" (Luke 24:11).

> But Peter arose and ran to the tomb; and stooping down, he saw the linen cloths lying by themselves; and he departed, *marveling to himself at what had happened.*
>
> —VERSE 12, EMPHASIS ADDED

And yet, after all of this, Peter still lost his vision.

PETER'S RESPONSE TO HOPELESSNESS

Peter had given up hope of ever being used by God again, and he decided to go back to what he was doing before he met Jesus.

> After these things Jesus showed Himself again to the disciples at the Sea of Tiberias, and in this way He showed Himself: Simon Peter, Thomas called the Twin, Nathaniel of Cana in Galilee, the sons of Zebedee, and two others of His disciples were together. Simon Peter said to them, "I am going fishing."
>
> —JOHN 21:1–3

Peter had decided to take up his old occupation. Yet, Jesus was determined to demonstrate His love for Peter and to clearly express to Peter that His purpose for him had not changed.

What Jesus does here is amazing. The rest of this incredible story is one of the most beautiful examples of God's love and grace in the Scriptures. (See John 21:1–19.) As we look at Jesus' intervention in

16

Peter's life at this point, it is important to understand what Jesus is about to do is for Peter's sake. Peter's failure had not changed Jesus' heart. God had not changed His mind toward Peter. Nothing new is about to be created here—except in the heart of Peter.

When Peter first met Jesus and was told he would become a "fisher of men," Peter had been fishing all night long without a single catch (Luke 5:5). Peter hadn't been alone that fateful day— James and John had been with him then, just as they are with him now when he goes fishing after Jesus' Resurrection. They have been fishing all night long this time, too, but not once have their nets felt the tug of struggling fish. Maybe in their boredom as they waited for their nets to fill they talked about the dramatic events of the previous week. The arrest of Jesus...the crucifixion...the way He miraculously appeared to them.

Certainly, Peter brought up his denial.

The sun's rays are now beginning to crest above the eastern horizon, painting the clouds a brilliant yellow. As the sky brightens, the disciples see the figure of a man standing on the shore. The stranger cries out to them, "Children, do you have any food?"

"Nothing," they reply.

"Cast your net on the right side of the boat, and I believe you will find some fish," the stranger responded.

They do, and the catch is so great that the nets begin to tear under the strain.

This scene begins to seem strangely familiar to Peter. Fishing all night long...empty nets...a stranger...a sudden catch of fish....At this point, John recognizes Jesus and says immediately to Peter, "Peter, it's Him! It's the Lord."

17

Instantly Peter's soul is arrested. His heart pounding and his mind racing, Peter lunges out of the boat and begins to swim frantically toward the man. The whole time he is swimming, these words flood his mind, *Jesus? Can it be Jesus? Can it really be Him? Like this? Again?*

By the time Peter and the disciples make it to the shore, Jesus already has a fire of coals burning. As Peter pulls himself from the sea and moves closer to Jesus, he can feel the heat from the fire. The early morning air is cold, and Peter immediately begins to warm himself from the flames that are twisting around the bright red coals. The fire also seems familiar. It looks a lot like the one he had stood next to on another night. A night he wished he could forget.

Neither Peter nor the disciples understand what is happening. They can somehow sense that there is a purpose for this event, but it's not yet clear what the purpose is.

After they have eaten, Jesus stands and turns to Peter. Every eye is fastened on the two of them. Slowly, taking a deep breath, Jesus asks, "Peter, do you love Me?"

"Yes, Lord, You know that I love You," Peter replies immediately.

"Then feed My lambs," Jesus says.

A few moments pass, and then a second time Jesus asks, "Peter, do you love Me?"

"Yes, Lord, You know...You *must* know that I love You."

"Then tend to My sheep," Jesus answers.

Several more minutes pass. Then Jesus turns to face Peter, locking His eyes on the disciple's face, and asks for a third time, "Peter, do you love Me?"

Peter is grieved. *How many times must He ask me?*

Peter thinks to himself. With his voice shaking with frustration, Peter declares more firmly than ever, "Lord, You know everything. Nothing is hidden from You. You must know how I feel. You know that I love You…"

Peter's words trail off as it suddenly becomes painfully clear what this moment is all about. A few nights before, three careless denials had stripped from him any hope of things ever being right again. And now, three times, Jesus is giving him an opportunity to declare his love. Tears well up in Peter's eyes as he looks up and sees Jesus standing there— smiling. "It's not over, Peter."

And it's not over for you, either. You may have failed God miserably. For years, you may have lived your life in a way that denied you ever belonged to Him. As a result, you may feel that God has given up on you. That He has thrown you away. That you could never find that place again of peace and joy, that place of knowing that you are forgiven and loved.

Or you may have been sexually, physically, or verbally abused in the past. Satan may have convinced you that you are damaged goods. Worthless and unworthy of true love and happiness. That is a lie! No matter

TURN AWAY FROM THE FLAMES OF THE PAST AND WARM YOURSELF BY THE FIRE OF TODAY'S VICTORIES.

what has happened, God has NEVER changed His mind about you. God's purpose for you need not be poisoned by your past. Your past doesn't determine your future—but how you respond to your past does.

Allow His Spirit to breathe in you again a fresh vision for your future. Let Him reestablish your worth and value. Go back to the place where you first heard Jesus' voice. The place where His purpose for you thundered in your soul. Let the sun begin to rise on the night of your past. Do you see Him? He is standing on the shores of your life today. He hasn't left; He hasn't forgotten you. He's made a bed of coals. You can turn away from the flames of the past, and you can begin to warm yourself by the fire of today's victories.

Shame? There's no place for it in the heart of God. What is God's answer to your shame? His love, which declares that you have immeasurable worth and value. What is God's answer to your guilt? The cross and His blood, which offers you forgiveness and cleansing.

3

Are You Imprisoned by Your Past?

OST OF THE TIME WHEN WE think about escaping our past we think in terms of those things that took place before we came to know Christ. The truth of the matter is that we are constantly dealing with the past. The past is what happened yesterday, this morning, or even five minutes ago. Consequently, you can see how vital it is that we constantly "forget those things which are behind." (See Philippians 3:13–14.) There are several emotional indicators that denote we may be imprisoned by our past. I want to deal with the three major ones.

EMOTIONAL WARNING SIGNS

ANGER

The first symptom of which to be aware is anger. Anger usually results when we feel that we have lost control of a situation or circumstance. Shame from the past will create thoughts of hopelessness, resulting in a sense that our lives are spinning out of control. Many times anger is the result. We become less tolerant of those around us. Even though anger is an attempt to control a situation or an individual with whom we are not pleased, it is actually an indication that we are not pleased with ourselves or with our own lives. A preacher friend of mine whom I consider a mentor once told me that he believed there was a direct correlation between anger and lying. Many times anger is an attempt to cover for areas of deception in our lives.

Outward bursts of wrath are easy to detect. But there is an expression of anger that is harder to recognize. It also needs to be viewed as a "red flag" to indicate a troubled heart. This form of anger is called *sarcasm.* Anger turned inward often expresses itself in the form of sarcasm. Many times this form of anger is veiled in humor. Even though it seems harmless, it has a detectable "edge." Sarcasm fires subtle darts of hidden criticism designed to demean its intended target.

In Ephesians 4:26–27 we read:

> Be ye angry, and sin not: let not the sun go down upon your wrath: neither give place to the devil.
>
> —KJV

This scripture is not giving a license to you and me to entertain the emotion of anger. The scripture is saying that when we are confronted with this damaging emotion we must deal with it before the day ends. If not, we will give place to Satan, allowing him to torment us with our own bitterness and disappointment as we lash out at those around us.

In my time of recovery, God began to show me the anger that had been a large part of my life for so many years. I had responded to the slightest infraction or disappointment with an explosive display of my displeasure, many times sending Bonnie and the children fleeing to a corner of the house to seek safety from my verbal tirades. As I began to deal with my anger, God graciously gave me several penetrating scriptures on this subject. One was Proverbs 14:17. It reads:

> A quick-tempered man acts foolishly, and a man of wicked intentions is hated.

I certainly had acted foolishly in my life. Another verse that God directed me to reads:

> He who is slow to anger is better than the mighty, and he who rules his spirit than he who takes a city.
> —PROVERBS 16:32

I was reminded of the fact that there have been men in history who ruled nations, but who could not rule their own lives or passions. Ultimately this lack of self-control cost them their kingdoms.

THE ELIJAH SYNDROME

A second emotional symptom of being imprisoned by our past is what I call the *Elijah syndrome.* This is a mind-set that leads to a victim mentality. It is extremely dangerous for anyone. I have seen it paralyze the effectiveness of many wonderful and sincere Christians. We see it demonstrated in the life of Elijah himself. This symptom is displayed in the infamous church service described in 1 Kings 18:21–40, the confrontation between Elijah and the prophets of Baal.

It was no ordinary service...

The crowd stood there frozen in suspense, anticipating what would happen next. It was a defining moment for everyone involved. The power of prayer put to the test...the authority of God's kingdom, for most there, stood in question.

The God that would answer by fire would be the one true God.

After hours of useless beseeching from the prophets of Baal, Elijah prayed. A burst of flames, and when the smoke cleared, Elijah's offering was nothing more than a black spot on the altar. The ground was licked dry by the tongues of heavenly fire, and four hundred fifty prophets of Baal lay motionless in a bloody heap.

Yet, by the time we read through to chapter 19, verse 9, we see a different Elijah.

> And there he went into a cave, and spent the night in that place; and behold, the word of the LORD came to him, and He said to him, "What are you doing here, Elijah?" So he said, "...I alone am left; and they seek to take my life."
>
> —1 KINGS 19:9–10

In no time at all, Elijah went from basking in the blinding light of God's glory to cowering in the corner of a damp and dark cave! In a self-imposed dungeon, Elijah became imprisoned by his own thoughts of hopelessness and despair.

Though the details may differ, there is a common thread that can explain what has brought many of us to the same place as Elijah. The key that led Elijah to his despair is revealed in what he said when God inquired as to why he was hiding in his sanctuary of self-pity. Look at what Elijah says in 1 Kings 19:10:

> I have been very zealous for the LORD God of hosts; for the children of Israel have forsaken Your covenant, torn down Your altars, and killed Your prophets with the sword. I alone am left; and they seek to take my life.

This statement is interesting in the light of God's response to Elijah concerning his lone crusade to defend God's kingdom. Notice what God said in verse 18:

> Yet I have reserved *seven thousand in Israel,* all whose knees have not bowed to Baal, and every mouth that has not kissed him.
>
> —EMPHASIS ADDED

When we are having difficulty in dealing with the past, even the slightest confrontation with any kind of obstacle can lead to one of the most effective lies from Satan—*that we are facing that difficulty alone.* The lie says that no one can understand what we are going through. Or the lie that causes us to think that no one else has it as bad as we do. As a result of this lie, we will find ourselves overcome with a victim mentality. We will begin to systematically cut ourselves off from those whom God has placed in our lives to aid and strengthen us with wise counsel.

When this begins to happen, we are then left to our own reasonings and perceptions. But compounding the problem is the fact that by the time we get to this point, those perceptions are usually distorted and inaccurate. When our friends attempt to encourage us or help us to see the situation more clearly, their words carry little or no weight.

ONE OF SATAN'S MOST EFFECTIVE LIES IS THAT WE ARE FACING THE DIFFICULTY ALONE.

It happened to me. One Sunday afternoon in 1988, I found myself emotionally overcome with self-hatred as a result of the secret sins of the past. My life was marked with anger and paranoia. I was sure that everyone hated me—a hatred I believed that I deserved. Through tears, Bonnie attempted to reason with me, pleading with me to see that these strangling emotions were a result of my own twisted perceptions. In my mind, her words meant little—I was convinced that she couldn't understand the demons with which I was struggling. And I certainly was not going to tell her.

Another time illustrates my distorted view of life. One Sunday morning we had just completed our time of worship. Once again my paranoia took over. As I stood to pray, I was sure that everyone in the sanctuary sat there looking at me with contempt. After I finished praying and the congregation took their seats, I turned to Ray Goolsby, one of the staff pastors and music director, and said, "These people hate the sound of my voice!"

I will never forget the look of concern on Ray's face as he asked, "Do you *really* believe that, Mike?"

"Yes, I do," I answered.

Then I turned, and under the guise of preaching the gospel, began to subject them to a barrage of rhetoric that only served to reveal my personal wounds and paranoia.

As preachers, many times what we think are sermons of great insight are really insights we have gained from unresolved conflict within our own souls. The stage becomes our platform to find some release from our own discontentedness and anger. The pulpit becomes our personal soapbox, and our doctrine becomes an elaborate form of reasoning that justifies our opinions and strengthens our positions.

In Elijah's situation, the power of God not only exposed the falsehood of Baal, but it also exposed some falsehoods in the mind of Elijah. One of those falsehoods involved not only Elijah's overexaggerated sense of importance, but also the fact that Elijah thought he stood alone in his trial. Anytime that Satan can get us to believe that our situation, difficulties, or temptations are unique, then he can dismantle us within our self-imposed state of isolation.

A LACK OF VISION

The third symptom of being imprisoned by our past is a *lack of vision*. This is characterized by our inability to see our lives correctly. This lack of vision will affect the sense of our own life's purpose and direction. A person who is enslaved by his or her past is unable to have a clear vision of the future. In Philippians 3:13, the apostle Paul states a twofold dynamic necessary in life—"forgetting those things which are behind and reaching forward to those things which are ahead." It is impossible to reach forward with vision if we haven't learned how to forget those things behind.

We see the power of vision in Habakkuk 2:2: "Write the vision and make it plain on tablets, that he may run who reads it." Vision brings a sense of purpose that will always provide direction for our lives. Without it, we become slaves to circumstances and opinions of men. Helen Keller was asked once what would be worse than being born blind. She quickly responded, "To have sight and no vision." When we have a clear sense of vision for our life's calling, we are less likely to expend our energy through useless distractions and unnecessary trends. Living in the past robs us of our vision for the future.

ESTABLISHING LIFE VALUES

A clear vision of our personal relationship with Jesus will enable us to run with direction and conviction. Through the neglect of our personal relationship with Christ, our vision of who and what we are in Him lacks the clarity and conviction necessary to make decisions that guard our integrity and bring God's best to our lives and family. Take a look at Proverbs 29:18:

Where there is no vision, the people are unre-
strained, but happy is he who keeps the law.

—NAS

A lack of vision results in what I refer to as a
"conflict of values." Just as our vision serves as a
compass, giving our lives clear direction, our values
serve a similar purpose. When we lose our vision,
we no longer have a clarity of values. God's Word
determines what our values should be. But for us to
experience the benefit of these values, they must,
through the work of the Holy Spirit, be internalized
and integrated into our daily decision-making
process.

Notice what the apostle Paul writes in Philippians
1:9–10:

And this I pray, that your love may abound still
more and more in knowledge and all discernment, that you may approve the things that are
excellent, that you may be sincere and without
offense till the day of Christ.

In these two verses Paul shares the secret to
finding the ability to make the right choices in life.

The Amplified Bible gives us additional insight
into what Paul is actually saying:

And this I pray: that your love may abound yet
more and more and extend to its fullest devel-
opment in knowledge and all keen insight [that
your love may display itself in greater depth of
acquaintance and more comprehensive dis-
cernment]…

—VERSE 9

Paul is saying that he's praying that out of their intimacy and greater depth of acquaintance with Jesus, their love would mature, resulting in keen insight into the affairs of their lives. Consequently, as he says in verse 10, this greater discernment would enable them to sense what is of *real value* in life. Discovering what is of real value is the secret to finding the strength to make "life-giving" choices.

THE POWER OF CHOICES

I cannot stress enough the impact our choices have in life. Our lives today are the culmination of the choices that we made yesterday. Even though there is forgiveness and restoration through the love of God, many situations bear consequences with which we must live—due to the choices that we have made. Our decisions not only affect our lives, but the lives of others. Actually, our decisions even affect the lives of those whom we have not even met.

I am reminded of a story that our pastor, Ted Haggard, shared one Sunday morning. Bonnie and I had just moved to Colorado Springs and had begun attending New Life Church. Pastor Ted shared a time when he was in college at Oral Roberts University. He had heard of the persecutions of the Christians that were taking place in the country of Albania. One form of persecution was to take the Christians out to the edge of the sea, place them in barrels, and then shove the barrels into the ocean. At this point, soldiers would begin to shoot at the barrels. As you can imagine, one of two things would happen. Either the Christians would be shot as the bullets ripped through the barrels, or if perchance the bullets missed them, the bullet-riddled barrel would begin to fill with water and sink, and these dear saints would drown. Often the persecutors would bring the family members of the Christians and force them to shoot at the barrels that held their loved ones.

Pastor Ted said that after hearing this, he stumbled out from his dorm to the campus and began to pray. One of his prayers was this: "God, please, someday use me to be part of the answer to the prayers rising up from those barrels." Pastor Ted said that in recent years there has been an increase in the number of people in Albania expressing an interest in the gospel. His point was that it would be arrogant to attribute the move of God to one ministry or organization. The truth of the matter is that there were people years ago who, in the face of great tribulation, chose not to become angry, bitter, or hopeless. Instead, they prayed for God's Word to have free course in the hearts of all Albanians. Now we are reaping the harvest for which others have sown.

This is the point—we are not alone. We are intrinsically connected as the body of Christ. In Hebrews 11:40 we read, "God having provided something better for us, that they should not be made perfect apart from us." Right before the fortieth verse, we read about the tremendous persecutions early saints endured for the sake of the gospel. Though they endured persecutions and perils we may never face—even martyrdom—verse 40 says that they should not be made perfect apart from us! We're in this thing together.

Hebrews 12:1 continues:

> Therefore we also, since we are surrounded by so great a cloud of witnesses, let us lay aside every weight, and the sin which so easily

ensnares us, and let us run with endurance the
race that is set before us.

The choices that we make today affect not only
our lives, but also the lives of the saints who have
gone before us. Their perfection is tied to the way
we run our race! The completion of what they
believed and for which they died is dependent
upon us finishing our course.

God will have a church, a people, who complete
their race. The question is, Are we going to play a
part in bringing His purposes to pass? The bottom
line is that your life matters. You are not insignificant! Regardless of your occupation in life, you can
make a difference. *Someone is counting on you to make
the right decision today.*

We are made in the image and likeness of God.
This involves many things. One of those things is
that we, like God, have a free will. I am convinced
that no matter how demonized a person might be,
that person never loses his or her ability to choose.
Also, God will never override a person's free will.

In the same way, Satan cannot usurp a man's
power of choice. We have the God-given ability, in
the face of circumstances, to choose what our
actions and thoughts will be. We are not animals.
We do not operate by instinct. God has given us His
ability to make life-giving decisions.

It is important to understand that our decisions
affect people we may meet five years from now.
You and I need to be in the place that God has for
us in years to come. We need to be there for the
people that He has assigned to cross our paths.

One of the results of the pain of the past is the
sense that our lives are no longer useful to God—or
anyone else, for that matter. Satan's desire is to strip

you from any sense of hope for your future through the guilt of the past. The truth of the matter is that regardless of what happened in your past, you have an opportunity to make a difference! You matter to God, as well as to others. It is never too late to choose to believe in His future for you.

THE POWER OF LIFE VALUES

It is clear that our choices carry powerful consequences. We may instinctively know that our life is a sum total of our choices. We understand that our life, like a ship on the ocean, has been piloted by the rudder of our decisions. Consequently, in our desire to undo the mistakes of yesterday, we desire to launch out into the depths of godly choices. Yet, most of the time we never get beyond the shores of good intentions. In order to discover the divine process for making the right choices in life, let's once again look at what the apostle Paul says in Philippians 1:10:

> That you may...approve and prize what is...of real value.
>
> —AMP

Within this scripture we see an amazing principle: Even as our lives are a reflection of our choices, *our choices are a reflection of our values.*

For example, Promise Keepers is a wonderful organization. Thank God for Bill McCartney's vision to inspire men everywhere to raise the standard of holiness and love. In each Promise Keepers meeting, men are challenged to commit themselves to seven promises. Thousands of men gather in stadiums all over the country, and with all the good intentions in the world, they promise to live their lives by these seven promises.

I guarantee that most of those men will break one, if not all, of those seven promises within a month. Is it because they were not sincere when they made the promises? Absolutely not! I suspect that these men were very sincere. But sincerity is not enough in life.

The mistake in exerting our strength to make right decisions is that we have the proverbial "cart before the horse." For years I was tormented with feelings of failure, never finding the strength to make the choices that I knew were necessary. I knew what choices I should make. I knew that I should spend more time with my children. I knew that I should love and esteem my wife over myself. But although I knew the things that I should be doing, even making promises to change, I found that I lacked the power to follow through with my good intentions.

According to Philippians 1:10, instead of focusing our attention on choices, we need to focus our attention on establishing life values. The secret is understanding that we do not have the will power to establish these values in our souls. In humility, we need to ask the Holy Spirit to breathe upon us and cement these values in our hearts. This is what Paul meant when he said that out of a greater depth of acquaintance with Jesus, we would have greater insight so that we may learn to sense what is of real value. This is where we begin to burn with His vision for our lives, which enables us to run with the necessary conviction. Then and only then will we find the power to make the decisions necessary that lead to releasing His life in our homes and families.

LIFE VALUES TRANSFORM GOOD INTENTIONS INTO GODLY DECISIONS!

Allow me to further explain how this has impacted my own life. Through my own selfishness and disobedience to God's Word, I nearly forfeited my relationship with Bonnie, Janae, and Josiah. Consequently, family has become an important value in my life. As God gave me a vision for my family, this vision translated into a concrete value. This value serves as a standard by which I evaluate and make decisions. I have regulated my schedule of speaking engagements primarily to weekends. As I receive invitations that would cause me to be away from home for long periods of time, it is not difficult for me to arrive at a decision: I will not do it. I have two teenagers at home. The time that Bonnie and I have with them equates to the "blink of an eye."

I believe that the teenage years are precarious. They are a real defining period of time. At this point in the life of our family, I need to be home and very much a part of my children's daily lives. Once our children are grown and out of the house, Bonnie and I will have plenty of time to travel and minister all over the world. Accepting invitations that keep me away from home for extended periods of time violates a very real value to which I am committed. *Family* is now more valuable to me than the temporary recognition that comes from ministry.

As another example—the most valuable possession that we have is our integrity. I traded my integrity for what probably added up only to a few hours of fleshly pleasure. As a result, integrity has now become an important value in my life. When I am presented with opportunities to compromise my integrity, it doesn't require long times of prayer

35

to choose honesty—regardless of the cost. A decision of truth may be painful now, but it will always bring great dividends in the future. *Integrity* is more valuable to me now than the temporary convenience that deception brings.

Our lives are simply a reflection of our personal relationship with Jesus. If we are experiencing the symptoms of burnout, it is because we have allowed the demands of life to crowd out our first priority—relationship with God.

In Mark 3:14–15 we read, "Then He appointed twelve, that they might be with Him and that He might send them out to preach, and to have power to heal sicknesses and to cast out demons." Our first calling is to be with Him and to know Him. In the past, whenever I read Scriptures or prayed, I had in mind the next sermon I would preach. Rarely, if ever, did I spend time in those disciplines for the purpose of enriching my own relationship with God. Yet, as I recovered the joy of His love for me and my relationship with Him, then I experienced the grace I needed to face the demands of life.

I want to challenge you to ask the Holy Spirit to establish His values for you and your family. Walk through that doorway of love and discover a greater intimacy with Jesus. Admit that you don't have what it takes—and never will—to live according to His standards. Once you do, a dynamic thing will take place. He will empower you to make the decisions that you always wanted to make, but for which you lacked the strength. You'll discover that your choices in life will begin reflecting your newfound values.

4

Barriers of Unforgiveness

I BELIEVE THERE ARE BASICALLY THREE ATTITUDES that empower the past to have a hold over our lives. These attitudes are doorways through which Satan will attempt to enter our lives with a deception that will, at best, neutralize our effectiveness. At its worst, it will completely destroy us. I receive hundreds of phone calls each year from people throughout the country who have been unable to escape the shadow of the past. Without exception, at least one of these three doorways was left open and unresolved. These attitudes are unforgiveness and judgment, insecurity, and duplicity. The next three chapters are devoted to exposing these areas of weaknesses and revealing the strength found in Christ to overcome them.

HEART CONDITION #1—
UNFORGIVENESS

The first attitude that chains us to the past is *unforgiveness*. Nothing will reveal the health of our relationship with God more than how we respond to those who have wronged us. Nothing has more potential for poisoning our lives and sabotaging our future than the way in which we handle life's offenses.

There are three basic misconceptions that serve as barriers to a life of forgiveness.

FORGIVENESS IS SIMPLY AN ACT OF THE WILL.

Once we are wronged, we are faced with the opportunity to make a decision to forgive—to release that person from their wrongdoing. This requires an act of the will, usually in the face of some very real and intense emotions of hurt, disappointment, and anger. Many believe that forgiveness is accomplished simply by this choice. We mistakenly assume that forgiveness is defined by our decision not to "return evil for evil."

But after we have made the choice to forgive, there must still be a resolution to the disturbing emotions of bitterness, anger, resentment, and sometimes even hatred. If not, we will find ourselves experiencing the dizzying effect of circling through the revolving door of our emotions, going from forgiveness to unforgiveness more times than we care to admit. I am convinced that many Christians merely tolerate the offender, rather than finding a place of genuine forgiveness toward them.

The first step in experiencing this work is to

realize our own inability either to forgive or to forget offenses. Achieving a resolution to these emotions takes a supernatural work of the Holy Spirit.

In Luke 17:4, Jesus speaks regarding forgiveness:

> And if he sins against you seven times in a day,
> and seven times in a day returns to you, saying,
> "I repent," you shall forgive him.

The disciples' response to this seemingly impossible command was "Lord, increase our faith...." In Matthew 18:22 Jesus takes this thought several steps further by saying that we must forgive "seventy times seven." This command simply means always—all the time, no matter how great the offense might be.

This command bankrupts any resources we have within our own humanity. It literally defies the laws of human nature to forgive endlessly those who have wronged us time and time again. Jesus intended this command to do just that—expose the impossibility of being able, within our own strength, genuinely to forgive those who have wronged us. It requires a supernatural work of the grace of God to love the offender and walk free from any emotions attached to the wrongdoing.

Let me further illustrate. Jesus said in a later verse, "If you have faith as a mustard seed, you can say to this mulberry tree, 'Be pulled up by the roots and be planted in the sea,' and it will obey you" (Luke 17:6). Confined to the laws of nature, it is impossible to uproot a tree with mere words. Yet within the context of this sentence, Jesus was saying that there is a grace available to us that transcends the laws of nature. Just as it would be impossible in our own strength to uproot a tree by a word, it is impossible to truly forgive. *Forgiveness is supernatural!*

By placing our faith in Jesus, there is a grace available to us that can transcend not only the offense, but all the painful, ugly emotions that bring us torment. Not only can we choose to forgive, but we can also experience God's love for the very one who brought us that pain.

Tom and Florence lived in Springfield, Illinois. Both were faithful members of a church in the city. Now that their children were out of the house, they were looking forward to the years they would have together as husband and wife, doing all the things they had planned to do. All that changed tragically one Saturday morning when Tom went to help a friend who was a landlord do repairs on some local apartments.

While Tom and his friend were working in a downstairs apartment, a man came storming in from the upstairs apartment. It was clear by his expression and by the glazed look in his eyes that he was high on some type of drug. Carrying a hammer and screaming about the noise coming from a construction site nearby, he grabbed the nearest person and slammed the hammer into his skull. Moments later, Tom's body lay lifeless on the floor.

Because of a few drug-crazed moments, Florence's life was drastically changed. In the aftermath of this horrible and senseless crime, the man was arrested, tried, and convicted. Sometime later, Florence visited the man in prison. She stood outside his cell explaining how he had robbed her of her lifetime mate, their retirement years together, and even her financial stability. Then she told him that she forgave him and handed him her husband's Bible as a gift. The killer was stunned by Florence's act of love. As a result, he read that Bible and gave his life to Jesus Christ.

I do not know the details of his sentence, but today this man is out of prison and preaching the gospel. He has returned to Springfield and has preached at the church that Florence still attends. It is amazing to me to think of Florence sitting in the congregation, listening to the man who killed her husband tell how he was transformed by the power of God's love through her simple act of obedience. "Impossible!" you say? Don't tell Florence; I don't think she knows any better.

> JUDGMENT IS PASSING SENTENCE ON SOMEONE'S LIFE AND ATTEMPTING TO IMPRISON HIM WITH OUR OWN OPINIONS.

I AM ONLY REQUIRED TO FORGIVE THOSE WHO ASK FOR FORGIVENESS.

Many come to this conclusion based on the verse in Luke 17:4 that says, "And if he sins against you seven times in a day, and seven times in a day returns to you, saying, 'I repent,' you shall forgive him." It is important to understand that the teaching on forgiveness in this verse is not all-inclusive.

When Jesus hung on the cross, there were seven statements that He made, one of which was, "Father, forgive them, for they know not what they do." None of the Gospel accounts tell of anyone coming to Him and repenting before Jesus made this statement.

In Ephesians we read, "And be kind to one another, tenderhearted, forgiving one another, even as God in Christ forgave you" (Eph. 4:32). How were we forgiven? Christ forgave us long before we asked for forgiveness or knew that we needed to be forgiven. True forgiveness must be based on our decision and upon the work of God that has been established in our hearts apart from and unaffected by the action and attitudes of others.

UNFORGIVENESS GIVES US CONTROL.

When we are wronged, the anger and disappointment that we experience comes from the feeling that we have been betrayed in some way. The anger is rooted in the feeling that we have lost control of some aspect of our lives to the offender. Our choice to hold on to the offense is actually a choice, through our anger, to regain control.

There is much about forgiveness within the parable of the unforgiving servant found in Matthew 18:22–35. Verse 34 says:

> And his master was angry, and delivered him
> to the torturers until he should pay all that was
> due to him.

In this verse Jesus teaches that when we attempt to imprison someone with our unforgiveness, it is actually we who are imprisoned and tormented. We have not *regained* control; we have actually *relinquished* control of our hearts and emotions.

When we do not resolve this issue of unforgiveness, we become victims of what I call "perceived offenses." If we do not find genuine forgiveness, we begin to interpret the actions of others as offenses—when actually they are not. We view the decisions and events around us as personal attacks. Our whole perspective in regard to our personal relationships will be jaded by our own hurts and disappointments.

It is so important for us to discover the security we have in God's love. Without that security, every relationship will be colored by past disappointments. Consequently, we will find ourselves sitting dangerously on the seat of judgment.

THE DANGER OF JUDGMENT

Jesus warns about the danger of sitting in judgment of others with His words of caution in Matthew 7:1–6:

> Judge not, that you be not judged. For with what judgment you judge, you will be judged; and with the measure you use, it will be measured back to you. And why do you look at the speck in your brother's eye, but do not consider the plank in your own eye? Or how can you say to your brother, "Let me remove the speck out of your eye"; and look, a plank is in your own eye? Hypocrite! First remove the plank from your own eye, and then you will see clearly to remove the speck from your brother's eye. Do not give what is holy to the dogs; nor cast your pearls before swine, lest

43

they trample them under their feet, and turn
and tear you in pieces.

Traditionally, we have interpreted verse 6 to
mean that we should not attempt to witness to
those who do not want to hear the gospel. If we
do, they will treat our words with contempt and
turn on us in some way. Actually, Jesus is still
talking about the danger of sitting in judgment over
someone's life. He is saying that when we climb on
someone else's back in judgment, we are taking the
pearl of God's mercy (that which is holy) and
giving Satan an opportunity to trample God's mercy
that has been covering our transgressions. We are
allowing Satan the opportunity to tear our lives to
pieces. Judgment takes us out of the covering of
God's mercy and grace, exposing ourselves to the
judgments of Satan against our lives. Satan is merci-
less, and he will not think twice about ripping our
lives and our families to shreds.

Remember the words of Jesus in Matthew:

Judge not, that you be not judged. For with
what judgment you judge, you will be judged;
and with the measure you use, it will be measured back to you.

—MATTHEW 7:1–2

One man felt it necessary to publicly judge
another man, and within a year his own private sin
was exposed to the public. Unforgiveness is defi-
nitely a *door* that we must, by the grace of God,
slam shut.

5

The Exaltation of Self

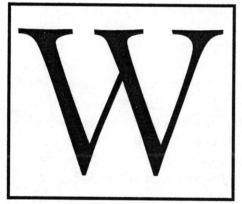

ITHIN A STATE-RUN institution for the physically and mentally impaired lived a little girl by the name of Annie. Even though Annie had the ability to speak, she rarely said a word. She was subject to violent bursts of wrath, lashing out with anger at anyone who attempted to reach out to her. After exhausting the resources available to them in that day, the institution finally labeled Annie "incurable." In order to keep others safe from Annie, and even to keep Annie safe from herself, she was housed in a private room located in the basement of this institution.

One worker, though, chose not to accept the sentence handed down to Annie. This young lady decided to take her lunch breaks in the basement, where she would read and talk to Annie on a daily basis. After some time, Annie began to show signs of improvement. Eventually, this young lady convinced the officials of the institution to give Annie another chance and move her back upstairs.

Ultimately, little Annie experienced total healing. When the time came for her to leave the institution, Annie decided to commit her life to helping others who had been labeled "impossible."

I have to say that I am impressed by this nameless "Samaritan" who so selflessly reached out to Annie. I must also admit that there was a time in my life that I would have been willing to do the same—*only if it would have resulted in the recognition of others.*

A story about my son, Josiah, brought this point closer to home. After school one day, Bonnie noticed that Josiah had not eaten his lunch. This continued for a week. Finally, Bonnie asked Josiah why he wasn't eating his lunch. Josiah explained that another boy in his class had fallen out of a tree, breaking both of his arms. This classmate needed someone to feed him his lunch each day. When the teacher asked for a volunteer, Josiah raised his hand. But by the time Josiah finished feeding the other boy, the lunch hour was over, and Josiah had no time to eat. Now, I am sure that the teachers would have allowed Josiah extra time to eat his lunch, *but he never told them he needed it.*

When I heard about this, I was struck with the recognition of an attitude that had marked my life. This attitude brought fear at the possibility of performing such an act of nobility—*without anyone noticing.* I have since realized that this all-consuming need for the attention of others comes from insecurity. *Deep-seated insecurity authorizes the past to continue to exert power over our lives.* If we are dealing with shame, then many times we find it necessary to create an image that we think will cause us to be accepted and valued by those around us.

HEART CONDITION #2—INSECURITY

For some, insecurity may demonstrate itself in becoming controlling and manipulative in relationships. For others it may demonstrate itself as a love of money. Or it may be seen in one who seeks to be empowered by sex. Whatever form it takes, insecurity will always demonstrate itself by one thing—*the exaltation of self.*

The result is selfish ambition, which is fueled by deep-seated insecurity. The danger of selfish ambition is that it is easily disguised as zeal for God's kingdom when, in fact, it is a desire to carve out a place of honor for ourselves. It is an attempt to add significance to our lives and to compensate for the shame we feel regarding the past.

Most of the time such an attempt takes place at the expense of other people. In Philippians 2:3, the apostle said:

> Let nothing be done through selfish ambition
> or conceit, but in lowliness of mind let each
> esteem others better than himself.

If we are unable to walk away from the past, then we become self-centered individuals. If the shame of the past is causing us to deal with a lack of worth and significance in our own lives, we will

47

be unable to truly esteem others better than ourselves.

SELFISH AMBITION

I want to identify three indicators of selfish ambition:

1. Desire for the recognition of men
2. Strife
3. A spirit of jealousy

DESIRE FOR THE RECOGNITION
OF MEN

At one point of His earthly ministry Jesus took
Peter, James, and John up on a mountain (Mark
9:2–7). As Jesus prayed, they witnessed His being
transfigured before them. His clothes and skin
became brilliantly white. Suddenly, Moses and
Elijah appeared and began to counsel with Jesus.
After this remarkable event, the three disciples and
Jesus proceeded down the mountain to the valley
below. As they approached the camp, Jesus saw
His other disciples gathered in a circle. It was
obvious by the commotion that the disciples were
in a heated debate among themselves. At the
center, Jesus saw a bewildered father standing hand
in hand with his boy at his side. As Jesus
approached the disciples, He discovered that the
disciples were arguing about whose fault it was that
they could not cast out the demon that had been
trying to kill this little boy.

Jesus took the boy aside and quickly drove out
the evil spirit. When the disciples asked Jesus why
they had been unable to cast out the demon, Jesus'

response was, "This kind can come out by nothing but prayer and fasting" (Mark 9:29).

As a side note, let me say that Jesus was not saying that if they prayed and fasted long enough, God would be moved to grant their request and deliver this boy from the demon. Prayer and fasting doesn't move God—He is not stuck! What Jesus was saying is that as we pray and fast, whatever is in us to which doubt and fear can attach themselves will be revealed and then purged, leaving only faith in the power of God.

Now, what takes place after this I find sadly amusing. The disciples had just experienced an embarrassing failure. A father had brought his boy to them to receive deliverance, and they were powerless to help the child. Yet after this event, as they walked toward Capernaum, they began to argue once again. This time they were debating who was the greatest among them! When they arrived in Capernaum, Jesus, knowing about their discussion on the road, confronted them by saying, "If anyone desires to be first, he shall be last of all and servant of all" (v. 35). Again later, Jesus found it necessary to once more say, "But many who are first will be last, and the last first" (Mark 10:31).

But the disciples had not yet conquered their desire for self-exaltation. Once again it surfaced:

> Then James and John, the sons of Zebedee, came to Him, saying, "Teacher, we want You to do for us whatever we ask." And He said to them, "What do you want Me to do for you?" They said to Him, "Grant us that we may sit, one on Your right hand and the other on Your left, in Your glory." But Jesus said to them, "You do not know what you ask. Are you able

to drink the cup that I drink, and be baptized with the baptism that I am baptized with?" They said to Him, "We are able."

So Jesus said to them, "You will indeed drink the cup that I drink, and with the baptism I am baptized with you will be baptized; but to sit on My right hand and on My left is not Mine to give, but it is for those for whom it is prepared."

—MARK 10:35–40

As you can see, James and John wanted a position of honor before men. Consequently, they were more than willing to share in Christ's persecutions, especially if it would assure them of this place of prominence. It is interesting that Jesus said *they would* experience His sufferings! But He could not promise them the positions of honor for which they were looking.

The question is not whether we will be rewarded for our faithfulness. The Scriptures are clear that God rewards those who have been counted faithful. The real question is one of motive. We need to ask ourselves, "Am I willing to endure hardship, even though it may not result in the position I desire? Am I willing to do the right thing, even if no one ever notices?"

In the past, my sense of worth and value were determined by the size of my church, the response of the people, and the recognition I received from those around me. This subtle attitude of insecurity usually did not prevent me from serving. As a matter of fact, I became driven in life, attempting to establish my worth through my many accomplishments. Afterward, when I didn't receive the recognition I felt I was due, I felt cheated and sometimes even angry. I am convinced that many times what we call a *pursuit of purpose* is really a *pursuit for significance.*

It is far too easy to do all the right things for all the wrong reasons. Many of us struggle with the fear that we will find ourselves "drowning in the sea of obscurity." If we are honest, what this life of obscurity signifies to us is a life void of the attention and approval of men.

BLINDED BY AMBITION, JAMES AND JOHN WERE WILLING TO TRADE THE PRESENCE OF GOD FOR A POSITION.

Jesus affirmed that James and John would be required to suffer for the sake of the gospel—yet without promise of their desired positions. Why? Because Jesus wanted their joy to be found in Him as their reward. Jesus wanted James and John to realize that their inheritance was standing in front of them.

Amazingly, as James and John stood in the very presence of the King of the universe they still strove for a place of honor among men. Look at what Jesus said in John 5:44:

> How can you believe, who receive honor from one another, and do not seek the honor that comes from the only God?

According to this scripture, it is impossible to have a vibrant, personal relationship with God if we place a higher importance on the honor that comes from men than on the honor that is received from God. Jesus knows what will be necessary to endure to the end—it will require our being counted faithful. He knows that the motive of our hearts must be free from self-assertion, seeking only to be satisfied by His pleasure.

How do we receive the honor of God? Very simply—through obedience. God's honor is bestowed upon us when we find our joy in simply doing His will. Jesus Himself said, "I can of Myself do nothing. As I hear, I judge; and My judgment is righteous, because I do not seek My own will, but the will of the Father who sent Me" (John 5:30). In John 6:38 Jesus said, "For I have come down from heaven, not to do My own will, but the will of Him who sent Me." In John 5:41 Jesus also said, "I do not receive honor from men." Jesus' honor was to do the will of His heavenly Father. This was His joy and delight.

STRIFE AND A SPIRIT OF JEALOUSY

In Mark 10:41 it says that the ten were displeased with James and John. The reason was that they were fearful that Jesus might grant James and John their petition, taking the place the ten desired for themselves. Ambition is always marked by jealousy. Jealousy comes from the fear that the accomplishments of others cheapen our sense of value. It is that feeling of anxiousness we experience when we hear about someone else experiencing the blessings of God or when we hear about the success of a fellow Christian. It often includes the secret delight we feel at the news of someone's failure.

An attitude of insecurity expresses itself many times in strife. In Mark 9:33, Jesus asked the disciples what they had been arguing about as they walked to the city of Capernaum. The Bible says the disciples were ashamed because they had been arguing about who was the greatest among them. Strife is a war of words that reveals a heart of ambition fueled by deep-seated insecurity. In Proverbs 13:10 it says, "By pride comes nothing but strife."

GREATNESS IN THE KINGDOM

As we continue looking at Jesus' confrontation with the ten disciples, we see that He continues to instruct His disciples concerning the driving force of self-centeredness, which springs from insecurity, saying:

> You know that those who are considered rulers over the Gentiles lord it over them, and their great ones exercise authority over them. Yet it shall not be so among you; but whoever desires to become great among you shall be your servant. And whoever of you desires to be first shall be slave of all. For even the Son of Man did not come to be served, but to serve, and to give His life a ransom for many.
>
> —MARK 10:42–45

Out of our own insecurity we will be driven to wield influence over other people as we attempt to secure our idolatrous position in their lives. Many times this will happen with little or no forethought of how our actions will affect the lives of others. This is the opposite of how the kingdom of God operates. The kingdom of God maintains an attitude of servanthood, which attacks self-centeredness, the focal point of any sin.

Even God in the flesh, when He came to this earth, came to serve. To sacrifice. To give His life a ransom for many.

I believe that Jesus is saying more than that we should not push our weight around in life. Jesus is also saying that in the kingdom of God, a man's life is not measured by the position he attains, but by the sacrifices he joyfully makes. In other words, the measure of our lives is not defined in terms of *position,* but rather in terms of *sacrifice.*

THE HEART OF A SERVANT

In Matthew 20:1–16 we can read the parable of the landowner who hired servants to work his field. The servants whom he hired initially agreed to work for a day's wage. Then in verses 3–7 we read:

> And he went out about the third hour and saw others standing idle in the marketplace, and said to them, "You also go into the vineyard, and whatever is right I will give you." So they went. Again he went out about the sixth and the ninth hour, and did likewise. And about the eleventh hour he went out and found others standing idle, and said to them, "Why have you been standing here idle all day?" They said to him, "Because no one hired us." He said to them, "You also go into the vineyard, and whatever is right you will receive."

So we see the owner of the vineyard still hiring others to work his field, even up to the end of the day. Yet it is at the conclusion of the story, when we see the owner begin to give out the wages, that we learn a powerful truth from Jesus.

> And when those came who were hired about the eleventh hour, they each received a denarius. But when the first came, they supposed that they would receive more; and they likewise received each a denarius. And when they had received it, they complained against the landowner, saying, "These last men have worked only one hour, and you made them equal to us who have borne the burden and the heat of the day."
>
> —MATTHEW 20:9–12

The men who had worked twelve hours were indignant at being paid the same amount as the workers who worked only an hour. In their minds this was a great miscarriage of justice. After all, they had worked the longest. They had earned the right for higher pay. If anyone deserved a bonus, they were the ones.

Have you ever experienced feelings of jealousy when you saw others promoted before you in God's kingdom? I know that there have been times when I have felt envy when I saw someone else receive recognition that I felt I deserved. When I would hear of a friend or acquaintance succeeding beyond me, I would immediately create a list of reasons why I should be experiencing at least as much success—if not more.

If we are not careful, we will even begin to murmur against God regarding this gross injustice. We will find ourselves blaming others because we have not moved forward in life. We will minimize the success of others as "a lucky break" or "being in the right place at the right time" or "playing office politics." This attitude causes us to assume the position of a victim. A victim mentality will keep us bound in the stranglehold of the past.

Now, back to the parable. Notice the response of the owner to the murmuring of these men.

> But he answered one of them and said, "Friend, I am doing you no wrong. Did you not agree with me for a denarius? Take what is yours and go your way. I wish to give to this last man the same as to you. Is it not lawful for me to do what I wish with my own things? Or is your eye evil because I am good?"
> —VERSES 13–15

God is saying, "Are you going to allow your heart to be defiled with jealousy because I show to another the same goodness I have shown you?" The bottom line is that the field we work in doesn't belong to us. It is God's. It is His kingdom that we are building. We are simply stewards, and the only thing that is required of a steward is that he is faithful. It is the *heart* of a servant that God considers great. The servant's heart is thankful just to be in the field.

A true servant isn't working for a certain reward. A true servant realizes that the Master is his reward. We are not in competition with each other. The prize doesn't go to the swiftest in this race. It goes to the one who runs faithfully and finishes his own personal course. It is the insecure laborer who always needs to be number one. It is the ambitious field hand who is always concerned about the status of the other workers. Jesus ended this teaching by saying, "So the last will be first, and the first last. For many are called, but few chosen" (v. 16).

The idea is not to take the position of being last in order to be first. Rather, the idea is, "I would like to be last, so that I am in the position to push the guy in front of me to the place of being first." Jesus said that the greatest in the kingdom is the servant of all.

I am convinced that Jesus' definition of greatness is radically different from ours. Greatness in God's kingdom is not necessarily measured by the size of our homes, the size of our income, or recognition from other men. It is measured by our obedience to His will and the value we place upon people.

Let's go back to the story of the nameless young lady who reached out to "little Annie." Years ago, Helen Keller was being honored for her contribution to the physically and mentally handicapped. As she gave her acceptance speech, she made sure to thank publicly the one lady to whom she attributed her success. Helen Keller called this woman her life-saver, the woman to whom she owed everything. That woman's name was Ann Sullivan—"little Annie." Thank God for the faceless young lady who started it all, simply because she chose to spend her lunch hour reaching out to one whom others had labeled "impossible." Even though we still do not know her name—God does. And that is what matters most.

A. W. Tozer has said:

> Many times man will share himself, he will even sacrifice himself for a desired end, but very rarely will he dethrone himself.[1]

It is this dethroning process that is difficult many times.

A song performed by Christian recording artist Clay Cross, titled "I Surrender All," has deeply challenged me to live in a greater place of surrender. The words of this song speak of the struggles of the songwriter to attain earthly gain, but he found the thrill of personal spiritual victory only after he learned to lay aside his strategies, ambitions, successes, trophies, and triumphs—everything—in order to run helplessly to God. With the songwriter, I have concluded that if God wants everything I have and am, then I surrender all to Him.

I hope that each of us will be willing to rise up and leave the camp of insecurity behind, seeking out that cleft in the rock where we discover His pleasure. Once we do, may we wedge ourselves within that place that *He* calls great, finding our worth and security in Him.

6

Living in Duplicity

HERE IS A STORY OF A FLEDGLING lawyer in Palmetto, Georgia, who was sitting in his new office waiting for his first client. When he heard the door open, he quickly picked up the phone and tried to sound very busy. The man could hear the young lawyer on the telephone saying, "Bill, I'll be flying to New York on the Mitchell Brothers deal; it looks like it is going to be a big one. Also, we need to bring Carl in from Houston on the Cimmeron case. Bill, you'll have to excuse me; someone just came in."

He hung up.

Turning to the man who had just entered, the lawyer said, "Now, how can I help you, sir?"

The man looked at him and smiled, saying, "I am just here to hook up the phone."[1]

When I heard this story, I was reminded of a scripture found in Proverbs 10:9 that says:

> He who walks with integrity walks securely,
> but he who perverts his ways will become known.

We can be sure that if we choose to live a life of pretense, at some point in time someone will be there to "hook up our phone." Regardless of how many people we are able to fool from behind our well-positioned masks of image and pretense, there is always someone who knows who we really are. It is so important to understand that image is *what* people think we are; integrity is *who* we really are. Sadly enough, many times it is easier to change people's opinions of us than it is to change who we really are.

HEART CONDITION #3— A DIVIDED HEART

When we refuse to walk away from the past, we become more concerned with image than with reality. The way people view us becomes paramount in our minds. If this attitude is not resolved by the Holy Spirit and the Word of God, we expend a lot of our energy in creating an image that we hope causes people to respect us. If we have not been able to experience true freedom from the past, then we continue to view ourselves in the specter of our failures. This, in turn, may cause us to project an image inconsistent with where we really are in life. Approaching life in such a way involves many inherent dangers.

It is imperative that we find the courage to live a life of transparency and honesty. The apostle Paul called this kind of existence a life of *simplicity.*

THE IMPORTANCE OF A
LIFE OF SIMPLICITY

In 2 Corinthians 1:12, the apostle Paul said:

> For our boasting is this: the testimony of our conscience that we conducted ourselves in the world in simplicity and godly sincerity, not with fleshly wisdom but by the grace of God, and more abundantly toward you.

In light of this scripture, I believe that there is a divine connection between choosing a life of simplicity and living a life of godly sincerity.

A life of simplicity is not a life of sackcloth and ashes and self-abasement. Literally, the word *simplicity* means "free from pretense and hypocrisy." Therefore, a life free from pretense automatically results in a life of sincerity. This principle works in the opposite as well. When we live in pretense and allow compromise in the smaller areas of our life, it will eventually result in compromise in the larger areas.

IRONING OUT THOSE FOLDS

In Luke 11:34 we read, "The light of the body is the eye: therefore when thine eye is single, thy whole body also is full of light" (KJV). The word *eye* is actually rendered "conscience." The word *single* means "having an absence of folds"—or a lack of duplicity in one's life. By this I am referring to those small

61

and sometimes undetectable areas of compromise, those attitudes that lead to the shading of truths in subtle areas and an embracing of double standards. For example, we don't *lie,* we *disinform*—we just don't tell the whole truth. Or when we communicate a story or situation, we always make sure to tell it in such a way that it puts us in the best light. This is what I mean by duplicity.

Now, Jesus is saying that if we, through the ministry of the Spirit and the Word, remove those areas of compromise and deception, our conscience will have the ability to guide us through life. Our eye will be single, and our whole body (our lives) will be full of light. It is God's desire that our lives be governed by the illumination of the Holy Spirit.

REVEALED TRUTH

THAT IS NOT

ACTED UPON

ALWAYS LEADS

TO DECEPTION.

Jesus continues His teaching: "But when thine eye is evil, thy body also is full of darkness. Take heed therefore that the light which is in thee be not darkness" (vv. 34–35, KJV). Jesus is saying that if we refuse to give up those small deceptions of convenience, our consciences will become dull and darkened. We will not be able to live our lives by the supernatural direction of the Holy Spirit. Instead, our lives will be governed by our own narrow reasonings and perceptions.

In many ways, we will not even realize the

dichotomy in which we are living. Nor will we realize the damaging effects of the choices we are making based on our unenlightened perceptions. That is why Jesus said in Luke 11:35, "Take heed therefore that the light which is in thee be not darkness" (KJV). It is possible to live within a self-deception. These seemingly insignificant areas of compromise open a doorway for Satan to deceive us, allowing larger areas of compromise that will rob us of our character. In James 1:22 we read, "Be doers of the word, and not hearers only, deceiving yourselves." Satan will attempt to extinguish our lamps through this duplicity and leave us groping around in the dark—left to our own limited understanding.

God is more concerned about our *character* than He is about our *reputation*. He knows that *reputation* is merely our value in the market of public opinion, whereas *character* is a demonstration of our implicit trust in Him. In reality, character is who we really are. There is a process by which character is developed. Unfortunately, in our desire for a life of ease, this opportunity often goes unrecognized.

GOD'S DIVINE CHAIN REACTION

In Mark 4:35–41 the disciples find themselves in the middle of the storm-tossed sea of Galilee. To make matters worse, Jesus, seemingly uncaring about their perilous plight, is asleep in the bow of the boat. I believe that in our usual emphasis of the obvious (Jesus' calming of the sea), we've missed the key that unlocks an understanding of a more vital issue of faith. Witness with me the storm-tossed sea of Galilee.

The storm must have come out of nowhere....

Even with the illuminating flashes of lightning, the driving rain made it almost impossible to make out the faces of the other men. The boat rocked violently as great waves swept over the sides. You could barely hear Peter's voice as he barked out the orders. Despite their Herculean effort, the boat was filling with water faster than they could bail it out.

Finally, in desperation they began to shake their leader out of His slumber. "Hey! We're drowning! We're not going to make it," they cried. "The boat is full of water, and we are going to die; what are You going to do about it?"

Slowly and deliberately Jesus climbed to the bow of the boat and, with a voice of calm authority, commanded the wind to cease. As suddenly as the storm started, it stopped. The clouds were pulled back like a curtain as slivers of the sun's rays began to warm their rain-soaked bodies. It was more than a calm. We'd have to call it a *great calm*. It was so quiet they could almost hear their hearts still beating wildly within their chests. The calm was so intense that the storm now seemed like a distant memory.

As wet strands of hair hung in His face, Jesus turned and met the gaze of His troubled men. With the same voice of authority, He lovingly yet sharply rebuked them, saying, "Why are you so full of fear? How is it that you have no faith?" *The disciples began to realize that somehow they had sacrificed a greater miracle for a lesser one.*

The same scenario has happened to many of us. We have heard His voice. We have stepped out in obedience, only to find ourselves right in the middle of a storm. Our boat is FULL, and it looks as if we are going under. Not only that, but it seems that Jesus is asleep. Our prayers seem to bounce off the ceiling. "Doesn't He care what I'm going through?" you ask. "Hey God, I think this would be a good time to wake up!"

It was the will of Jesus to get to the other side of the lake. But it was not His original plan to calm the storm to get there. Let me ask you: What would have been a greater miracle? Would it be Jesus calming the storm? That could have been easily explained away as some freak act of nature. How about a boat full of water bumping up against the shore, defying those laws of nature?

Better than those examples, how about a group of men who decided to allow the words of Jesus to speak louder than the storm? They were looking for peace—He was in the boat. After all that the disciples had seen and heard, Jesus wanted His word to be enough for

CHARACTER IS REVEALED BY WHAT WE DO IN TIMES OF ADVERSITY; INTEGRITY IS REVEALED BY WHAT WE DO IN TIMES OF SUCCESS.

them. He calmed their storm, but He wanted His word to calm their hearts. He stopped the winds, but they missed an opportunity to have His character fashioned in them as they identified with His.

Don't misunderstand me. I am not saying that God is the author of our tribulation and persecutions!

I am saying, according to Romans 5:3–4, that there is a divine chain reaction that takes place when we are faced with the storms of life. "And not only that, but we also glory in tribulations, knowing that tribulation produces perseverance; and perseverance, *character*; and character, hope…" (emphasis added). As a matter of fact, a person that constantly deals with hopelessness is a person who lacks character.

It is not the storms of life that bring character in our lives. Our decision to trust Him in the midst of our storms opens the opportunity for our lives to be established with *character*. Paul was saying that we are not going to get by with escaping tribulations and hardships in this life. They are a fact of existence on this planet. So we might as well glory in them. Not glory *for* them, but glory *in* them. Why? Because as we trust in the integrity of His Word, clearing the storm, we will have experienced the work of His character within us—not to mention the gasps of disbelief from those who are looking on. When they see you overcoming a storm that would kill a normal man or woman, you can tell them what God's Word says. And, my friend, there is nothing normal about that. Character has the ability to ignite hope not only in our hearts, but also to ignite hope in the hearts of others.

A LIFE OF CHARACTER IS DEFINED BY DAILY CHOICES OF TRUTH

In March 1990, Dr. Robert McQuilken announced his resignation as president of Columbia Bible

College. He was leaving to care for his wife, Muriel, who was suffering from the advanced stages of Alzheimer's disease. Within Dr. McQuilken's resignation letter is a powerful key to preparing one's life for making decisions of integrity. He writes:

> My dear wife, Muriel, has been in failing mental health for about eight years. So far I have been able to carry both her ever-growing needs and my leadership responsibilities at CBC. But recently it has become apparent that Muriel is contented most of the time she is with me and almost none of the time I am away from her. It is not just "discontent." She is filled with fear—even terror—that she has lost me and always goes in search for me when I leave home. So it is clear to me that she needs me now, fulltime.
>
> Perhaps it would help you to understand if I shared with you what I shared at the time of my resignation in chapel. The decision was made, in a way, forty-two years ago when I promised to care for Muriel "in sickness and in health...till death do us part." So, as I told the students and faculty, as a man of my word, integrity had something to do with it. But so does fairness. She has cared for me fully and sacrificially all these years; if I cared for her the next forty years I would not be out of debt. Duty, however, can be grim and stoic. But there is more; I love Muriel. She is a delight to me—her childlike dependence and confidence in me, her warm love, occasional flashes of wit I used to relish so, her happy spirit and tough resilience in the face of her continual distressing frustration. I do not have

to care for her; I get to! It is a high honor to care for so wonderful a person.[2]

It would be a mistake to assume that a decision of this magnitude was an isolated choice—independent of smaller, daily decisions of truth. The choices we make today prepare us for the grand decisions of integrity later.

Jesus is in the garden, facing His greatest temptation ever (self-preservation). The shadow of the cross is looming over Him. He can already begin to feel the tongues of hell's fire and the fury of His archenemy, Satan. As Jesus wrestled with His own humanity, He prayed, "O My Father, if it is possible, let this cup pass from Me; nevertheless, not as I will, as You will" (Matt. 26:39). I do not believe that this is the first time that Jesus prayed this statement. Actually, I believe He prayed this every day of His life. In all reality, this prayer represented Jesus' entire life and ministry. All through His life, Jesus resisted the sin of self-assertion. He said Himself that He only spoke what He heard the Father say and only did what He saw the Father do. Therefore, when it came down to the final decision with the future of all humanity hanging in the balance, Jesus had the foundation of a lifetime of obedience and relationship with His Father from which to draw. Yes...there was no other viable choice..."Not my will but thy will be done!"

What decisions are you making on a daily basis? What are your priorities? Are they the same as the Father's? Are the decisions you are making now going to bring His glory to your life twenty years from now? What kind of effect are your decisions having on your life and family? The prize does not go to the swiftest, but to the one who crosses the finish line. How we finish is as important as how we begin. Let's make the choices necessary to finish our course *strong*. Someone else's life may depend on your choices. Your character certainly does.

7

The Shadow of Your Past in the Light of the Cross

I N THE EARLY SEVENTIES, TWO SISTERS WERE abducted by two men as they came out of a convenience store in Wyoming. The two men drove the two girls to a canyon bridge, where they brutally beat and raped the older girl. Somehow she talked the men out of doing the same to her younger sister.

When these men had finished with their crime, they threw both girls over the bridge that hung suspended one hundred twelve feet above the river.

The younger sister was killed instantly. The older sister, landing in deeper water, swam to shore and wedged herself between two large rocks, shivering violently from fear as much as from the cold. The next day she was rescued. Her wounds were treated. Her kidnappers were arrested, tried, and sentenced, but she was never able to escape that canyon of darkness.

Nineteen years later, the older sister drove back to that same bridge. With her two-year-old daughter and boyfriend at her side, she sat at the edge of that bridge and wept. She looked over that canyon that she was never able to escape, reliving the horror of those hours. The boyfriend thought it best to take the child to the car. That is when he heard the splash of shallow water. She had finally surrendered to the canyon that had so cruelly branded her soul, sacrificing herself on the jagged stones of the past.

Sadly, there are a lot of people like that older sister out there, both male and female, wandering around canyons of hopelessness, shame, and guilt. They may have been flung over that precipice through their own wrong choices or through the evil choices of others. Ultimately, it doesn't matter how they got there. If they stay, the result is the same—death. Death to dreams, hope, and to the future.

At best they become the walking wounded. Spiritually limping through life. Allowing the past to poison their minds and every relationship they have. As much as they try to outrun those tormenting thoughts, they find themselves driving back to that bridge, looking out over that canyon in their minds, paying some sort of twisted homage by reliving the hurt, failure, and disappointment again, and again, and again. As if by rehearsing it, the sordid story will come out differently.

What are the things in your past that you have had difficulty overcoming?

REDEEMED FROM SHAME

The cross declares that you are redeemed from the shame and guilt of the past. In his preaching, the apostle Paul continually referred to the cross of Christ.

> But God forbid that I should boast except in the cross of our Lord Jesus Christ, by whom the world has been crucified to me, and I to the world.
>
> —GALATIANS 6:14

One message that the cross declares is that *the past need not overshadow our lives.* For us to be able to escape our past, we must begin to see the actions of our past in light of Jesus' supreme act of love on the cross. It is as we understand His finished work that our past begins to lose its hold over our lives.

Colossians 2:14 describes what Jesus accomplished through His sacrifice on the cross:

> ...having wiped out the handwriting of requirements that was against us, which was contrary to us. And He has taken it out of the way, having nailed it to the cross.

The word for *handwriting* in the Greek literally means "holograph." This word, though, eventually evolved to mean "a certificate of debt." In New Testament times documents were written on papyrus. The ink was made of soot, mixed with gum, and diluted with water. As a result, the ink had no acid in it and would not stain the paper. No matter how long the document had been written, a wet sponge could completely erase the writing. However, this is not how a debt was usually canceled. Normally, if a judge decided to cancel a certificate of debt, he would place a large *X* on the document, crossing out the debt. Consequently, the record of the debt would still be visible and subject to examination.

When he referred to what Jesus accomplished on the cross, the apostle Paul does not say that Jesus "crossed out" the debt we owed. Paul says that Jesus "wiped out" the handwriting of requirement that was against us. This means that the debt we owed was erased, obliterated, gone forever! Sponged over and the slate wiped clean. It is as if the debt never existed. This is what happens when we receive His forgiveness. We are not only forgiven, but what we have done is forgotten in the mind of God. Psalm 103:12 says, "As far as the east is from the west, so far has He removed our transgressions from us."

In Galatians 3:13 we read, "Christ has redeemed us from the curse of the law, having become a curse for us (for it is written, 'Cursed is everyone who hangs on a tree')." Death by the cross was done in a public place to bring shame upon the convicted criminals. As Jesus hung on the cross, He redeemed us not only from the *power* of sin, but also from the *guilt* of sin as well. In Hebrews 12:2 we read, "Looking unto Jesus, the author and finisher of our faith, who for the joy that was set before Him endured the cross, despising the shame, and has sat down at the right hand of the throne of God." Clearly, Jesus not only became sin, bearing its penalty, but He also bore the shame and guilt that sin brings.

THE CROSS DECLARES A RIGHTEOUSNESS THAT IS NOT OUR OWN

In Philippians 3:13 Paul writes, "Brethren, I do not count myself to have apprehended; but one thing I do, forgetting those things which are behind and reaching forward to those things which are ahead..." Paul was actually saying that he was assigning his past to a place of oblivion where he would no longer define who he was by what he had done. Paul's secret to being able to let go of yesterday came from an understanding of the basis of his righteousness.

Notice what it says in Philippians 3:3: "For we are the circumcision, who worship God in the Spirit, rejoice in Christ Jesus, and have no confidence in the flesh." Most Christians place their trust in how they perform in establishing a right standing before God. For example, if we feel that we have performed well, then we have a sense of confidence before God. If we have failed in our Christian walk, then we often find ourselves under a weight of anxiety and hopelessness. This response simply reveals that we have placed our confidence in our "flesh," attempting to secure our own brand of righteousness. It is a form of spiritual pride to place more value on what we have done than what Jesus did through His finished work. The most difficult thing for us to do is to embrace this truth and place more value on the sacrifice of Christ than on what we have done.

As long as we try to relate to God through our actions, we will always find it difficult to escape our past. For example, in Romans 4:4–5 we read, "Now to him who works, the wages are not counted as

75

grace but as debt. But to him who does not work but believes on Him who justifies the ungodly, his faith is accounted for righteousness."

Let me share a story that I think will further illustrate this scripture.

When I first moved to Chicago, I had a very difficult time getting a job. My degree was in theology, and all of my experience was in the pastoral ministry. Consequently, this did not put me in big demand in the secular work force. I soon discovered that the only jobs I was able to secure were sales positions. This meant that I was paid on commission. I received a percentage of the amount of product that I sold. My first sales job was working in an upper-scale men's clothing store.

I can remember coming home one Wednesday afternoon and excitedly telling Bonnie how well I did that day and how much money I had made. I shared with her the details of every sale. We praised God together and rejoiced over my success that day. What I didn't realize was that as we were rejoicing, customers were coming in that evening to return clothing I had sold them in previous weeks. That particular night, each customer was conscientious enough to bring their sales slip, which contained my employee number. As a result, each item returned that night that I had previously sold was subtracted from my total commission.

When I showed up for work the next morning I discovered that I was four hundred dollars in the hole. This meant that I had to sell four hundred dollars worth of inventory just to start at zero. What a frustrating feeling that was. I felt that the harder I worked, the farther I fell behind.

This is the way a lot of Christians feel! Many times we are troubled by a sense of debt—the feeling of never quite doing enough. We have become overwhelmed with the frustration of never praying enough, reading the Bible enough, or serving enough. It seems that the harder we try to please God through our works and effort, the farther away He seems to be.

The reason we feel that way is because what we do is really never enough. God will not allow us to sense His grace over our lives or to sense the pleasure of His love if we attempt to relate to Him through our works. God is much more concerned about a relationship with us than with what we can do for Him. Our righteousness is not based upon *what we do,* but in *whom we believe.*

The only way we can really live beyond our past is by refusing to define who we are by what we have done or by what has been done to us. If we continue to find our identity in our failures, then we will always be imprisoned by our past. There is no way that you can change your past. It is impossible to alter the things that we have done.

If we put our trust in our ability to find a sense of righteousness by our actions, the past will continue to have a hold on our lives. Only by recognizing the weakness of the flesh can we realize the futility of our past actions. The key to walking away from the past is learning to *enjoy* a righteousness that was not ours, nor could it ever be established by us.

GOD'S GRACE EMPOWERS US TO LIVE GODLY

If we really believe that Christ is our righteousness—and it is only because of Him that we can stand right before God—then we will begin to live that way. People who think that they have an understanding of grace, but continue to live by the selfishness of their own flesh, really do not understand God's grace at all. Notice what it says in Titus 2:11–12:

> For the grace of God that brings salvation has appeared to all men, teaching us that, denying ungodliness and worldly lusts, we should live soberly, righteously, and godly in the present age.

God's grace is not a blanket thrown over our lives to prohibit God from seeing our acts of disobedience. Rather, God's grace will quicken faith in the power of the cross and in the blood of Jesus. His grace will cause us to lose sight of *ourselves* in light of *His* glory and love, resulting in the transformation of our souls.

As we discover our identity in Him, our lifestyles will begin to reflect our new sense of identity. When we see ourselves established in His righteousness, we will live as one who loves righteousness and hates iniquity.

Even though we may feel a sense of responsibility for what we have done, if we allow ourselves to feel guilty, then we will continue to identify with our past actions, elevating them to a higher place than the cross. As a result, we will polarize ourselves from the sense of God's love, deliverance, and sustaining power.

THE CROSS DELIVERS US FROM A VICTIM MENTALITY

Another reason that it is crucial for us to realize the basis of our righteousness is to avoid becoming paralyzed by a victim mentality. We cannot afford to be seduced with the idea that we are victims of circumstance. If we do not escape the past by the power of the cross, we will be tempted to blame everyone else for the condition of our lives.

In John 5:1–8 we have the story of Jesus healing the crippled man at the pool of Bethesda. There are several interesting facts within this story that shed some light on an enemy called "the victim mentality."

As Jesus approached the pool of Bethesda, he asked the lame man this question, "Do you want to be made well?" Jesus wanted to know in what the lame man had placed his faith. Had this lame man resigned himself to his infirmity? Did he really want to be made well, or did he enjoy the freedom from responsibility that his sickness afforded him?

Notice that the crippled man never directly answered the question. His reply exposed his "victim mentality." When asked if he wanted to be made well, he began to complain that he had no one to put him in the water as the others did. "It is someone else's fault that I am still sick. If only someone else would do 'such and such,' I could be a whole person." This attitude has invaded the minds of many believers, paralyzing them from a joyful, productive life.

The truth of the matter is that the moment we received Jesus as our Savior, we were redeemed from the authority of darkness and translated into His kingdom. We are born again! We have the name of Jesus. We have His nature. We have His seed of greatness! The Greater One lives within us.

You may have been abused in some way during your childhood—physically, mentally, or sexually. Your life may be in shambles because of your own wrong choices. Or, you may have found yourself in an abusive relationship with a spouse, family member, or friend. I do not want to minimize the pain that you feel. But His grace and love are bigger than what happened yesterday.

In John 1:12–13 we read, "But as many as received Him, to them He gave the right to become children of God, to those who believe in His name: who were born, not of blood, nor of the will of the flesh, nor of the will of man, but of God." This means that regardless of our background, we are born of His Spirit; we have the capability to take on the characteristics of God's personality, passions, and character.

The question we must ask is, With whom are we going to identify? If we identify with the past—the symptoms, the lack, and the fear—we will imprison ourselves with our own infirmities. We will be impotent in life, always seeing ourselves as the one in need instead of as the one who is used by God to be His expression of life, love, and power!

JESUS' DEATH ON THE CROSS OUTSTRIPS AND OUTWEIGHS ANYTHING YOU HAVE EVER DONE OR ANYTHING THAT HAS BEEN DONE TO YOU.

Romans 5:17 tells us that we can reign as kings in this life through the grace of God.

> For if by the one man's offense death reigned through the one, much more those who receive abundance of grace and of the gift of righteousness will reign in life through the One, Jesus Christ.

As we choose to identify with the Greater One, some startling things take place:

- Courage replaces timidity.
- Confidence replaces shame.
- Faith replaces fear.
- Love conquers bitterness.

As we place our faith in His eternal sacrifice, we can experience power over the influence of our past. Choose to see yourself the way God declares you to be. Yesterday is over! There is no person or circumstance that can imprison you.

What Jesus did on the cross outstrips and outweighs anything that you have ever done or anything that has been done to you.

8

The Blood and Your Past

E HAVE HEARD MUCH IN past years about the wonderful covenant of blood that exists between the Father and the Son and the benefits we share as heirs of Jesus. Though this is a great truth, it is only one facet in the beautiful diamond of redemption. As we look at what the Scriptures say about the blood of Jesus, I believe the Spirit will reveal to us the significance of the blood as it applies to our past. For us to really understand the importance of the blood regarding our past, as well as understand the power we can experience from the blood for our present, we must to go back to the beginning.

> And the LORD God formed man of the dust of
> the ground, and breathed into his nostrils the
> breath of life; and man became a living being.
> —GENESIS 2:7

The King James translation says that man became a living "soul." Notice that once Adam had been created, he had everything physically necessary to live, yet he stood lifeless. It was not until God breathed His breath into Adam's nostrils that Adam had life. The moment that God released His breath into Adam, God's life came into him. I believe it is important to note a verse we find in the Book of Leviticus, which gives us some additional insight into the creation of man.

> The life of the flesh is in the blood.
> —LEVITICUS 17:11

According to this scripture, it is blood that gives life to the flesh.

As Adam stood lifeless, the Bible says that the Spirit of God blew through Adam, creating blood in Adam, thereby giving him eternal life. Every part of Adam was created from this earth except the very thing that would give his flesh and soul life—blood. Adam's blood had nothing to do with this earth. It was divine, created by the Spirit, straight from the loins of God. This is a vital truth, for it was this blood and God's Spirit that enabled Adam to fellowship and relate perfectly with God. Adam was truly born from above! Adam became a living soul. That means that Adam thought like God; he experienced the passions God experienced. It was God's life, flowing through the blood that enabled Adam to enjoy intimacy with his Father.

GOD'S GLORY AND THE BLOOD

As we continue this story from the Book of Genesis, we see that Adam and Eve disobey God, eating the fruit of the tree that was forbidden to them. In Genesis 3:7 we read:

> Then the eyes of both of them were opened, and they knew that they were naked; and they sewed fig leaves together and made themselves coverings.

Adam and Eve saw that they were *naked,* and they sewed fig leaves together to hide their nakedness. When Adam and Eve sinned, their blood became defiled. They became mortal, and immediately God's presence lifted from them. It had been the work of the Spirit that imparted God's life-giving blood into Adam. The blood brought God's presence in and upon Adam and Eve.

In the Old Testament the word *glory* represents God's Spirit and presence. In the Hebrew, the word *glory* is the word *chabod,* which is translated "weight" or "substance." God's presence rested upon Adam and Eve through the vehicle of blood that brought weight and substance to their lives. His Spirit gave Adam and Eve their sense of substance and significance. At the time of their disobedience, Adam and Eve were clothed entirely by God's glory—by His presence! But God Himself had said, "If you eat of this tree, you shall surely die." After their disobedience, their eyes were opened, and they sensed their nakedness. It was not the absence of clothing that caused them to be naked. *It was the absence of His presence.* By their own admission, even after they made coverings they knew they were still naked (Gen. 3:10).

85

There are many today who still try to fashion coverings for themselves in an attempt to cover their sense of incompleteness and emptiness. Whether they do so by obtaining wealth, power, position, the approval of man, drugs, or illicit sex, all of these are futile and leave us empty, afraid, and full of shame. Friend, there is no substitute for God's presence and glory in our lives!

In this account in Genesis we see the vehicle by which God restored His Spirit back to those who bear His image. Genesis 3:21 reads, "For Adam and his wife the LORD God made tunics of skin, and clothed them." Adam and Eve were not clothed until God Himself went out and by His own hand slew an animal. Yet even in this symbolic act, it was not the coats of skin that clothed them; it was the blood that had to be shed that brought God's presence to rest upon them.

My friend, from the beginning God ordained that it would be through the shedding of blood that He would restore His glory back to His people. It would be accomplished through the shedding of the blood of the perfect Adam, who would destroy the power of sin and cause His Spirit to dwell within man. Thus man's relationship with his Creator would be restored.

For example, what was the difference between Cain's sacrifice and Abel's? (See Genesis 4:1–8.) They both brought their firstfruits to God, yet God accepted Abel's sacrifice and rejected Cain's sacrifice. The difference was that Cain ignored God's prescription for worship. Cain most certainly had been told the story of his parent's disobedience many times. Cain knew plants could not atone for sin, but he used them anyway. Cain knew that the shedding of blood was required. In Hebrews 9:22

we read, "And according to the law almost all things are purified with blood, and without shedding of blood there is no remission."

Cain insisted on bringing a bloodless sacrifice before God. Cain wanted to worship God according to *his way*, not *God's way*.

Abel's worship to the Lord included the necessary ingredient of the shedding of blood, which was the type and shadow of what would be God's ultimate sacrifice—the life of His own Son. All through the Scriptures we see a relationship between the Spirit and the blood. Every time blood was shed in worship, God's glory was manifested.

The Bible says that during the time of worship when Solomon dedicated the temple, the number of sheep and oxen that were slain was so great that they could not be numbered (1 Kings 8:5). As a result we read:

> And it came to pass, when the priests came out of the holy place, that the cloud filled the house of the LORD, so that the priests could not continue ministering because of the cloud; for the glory of the LORD filled the house of the LORD.
>
> —1 KINGS 8:10–11

It is clear that through the blood God would cause His presence to rest upon man. In the New Testament we can see that it was through the blood of Christ that God's presence could once again dwell within man.

THE BLOOD'S POWER

God Himself prophesied in Genesis 3 of a seed that would come from the same being that Satan deceived—woman. (See Genesis 3:15.) Satan would bruise the heel of this seed, but the seed would crush Satan's head. Thousands of years later a woman named Mary gave birth to this seed—Jesus—referred to in 1 Corinthians 15:45 as "the last Adam." Being conceived by the Holy Spirit, His blood was not of this earth. It was divine and supernatural; it carried within it eternal life. Once again the Father has a perfect man on the earth.

Notice what the Scriptures say about the blood of Jesus in Hebrews 9:13–14:

> For if the blood of bulls and goats and the ashes of a heifer, sprinkling the unclean, sanctifies for the purifying of the flesh, how much more shall the blood of Christ, who through the eternal Spirit offered Himself without spot to God, cleanse your conscience from dead works to serve the living God?

Christ willfully took His life of perfect obedience and shed His blood on the cross. The blood represents His life of humility and surrender to the will of the Father. The blood of Jesus goes beyond just canceling out the wrong actions of man. According to the Scripture, the blood carries with it the power to purge from man the inward bent toward rebellion. Only this blood could drive beyond the veil of the flesh, destroying its right to rule us. The blood goes beyond atoning for the sins of the flesh—it actually purges the conscience, infusing man with God's nature, invading man with eternal life. As a result, this blood enables man once again to enjoy unbroken fellowship with the One whose image he bears. This is a foundational truth of the blood of Jesus. As I place my faith in the power of His blood, I can expect deliverance from sin's power.

A GUILTY CONSCIENCE

Not only does this purging work of the blood mean that I can live above the power of the flesh, but the purging of dead works also means that I can live free from the sense of guilt and shame that sin brings. God, through the blood, dealt with sin as a whole. Not only the *power* of sin, but also the *guilt* of sin.

Christ's blood will purge our conscience from dead works to serve the living God (Heb. 9:14). The *conscience* is that part of us that is able to discern between right and wrong. The conscience also testifies of the state of the heart. For example, the conscience will speak to our soul when we have lived life in a manner of godliness and holiness.

Notice what the apostle Paul says in 2 Corinthians 1:12:

> For our boasting is this: the testimony of our conscience that we conducted ourselves in the world in simplicity and godly sincerity, not with fleshly wisdom but by the grace of God, and more abundantly toward you.

Regardless of the accusations that were brought against Paul and his fellow ministers, Paul knew that he had no reason to be ashamed. His conscience testified to him that he had conducted himself in godliness. In the same manner, when we have lived outside the boundaries of God's Word, it is the conscience that the Holy Spirit uses to convict us.

Satan will attempt to pervert this process. We will never be perfect in life, and Satan uses the occasions of imperfection to bring shame to our conscience. The emotion that follows is guilt, which is the counterfeit of conviction. Let me explain what I mean. *Guilt* is more than understanding our responsibility for our own behavior. It is an overwhelming sense of self-reproach. This results in a sense of inadequacy, which causes us to identify with the actions of the past so completely that we despair of ever living beyond our failures. Consequently, we have a constant sense of foreboding before God. We begin to believe that God has rejected us and removed His love and grace from our lives.

Another phenomenon also takes place in our lives regarding guilt. Not only can the emotion of guilt come from actual sins we have committed, it can come also as the result of perceived sins. By this I mean that we can experience a sense of guilt but not really be able to identify the source of our guilt. Many Christians look for a sense of forgiveness from God, yet they never find it because of perceived guilt. They believe God *has not,* and *will not,* forgive them. But God cannot forgive because they have done nothing wrong!

This vague sense of guilt without a source is the primary difference between *guilt* and *the conviction of the Holy Spirit.* When the Holy Spirit brings conviction, it is always specific. As God enlightens His Word to you, you know exactly where your thoughts or actions have strayed. He brings specific conviction for specific disobedience.

In addition, the conviction of the Holy Spirit always results in hope—hope of freedom as well as an assurance of His love and mercy. Guilt results in despair. It is accompanied with thoughts such as, *I will never be free from these sins.* Or, *I am sure that God has abandoned me forever.* Guilt steals our hope and causes us to hide from God. Guilt originates in hell and is spawned by Satan.

Conviction is a gift from heaven and is birthed by the Spirit. Conviction causes us to run toward God; guilt causes us to run from God. Conviction results in being God-conscious; guilt results in being self-conscious. The sense of guilt robs us of our peace and confidence before God.

What then is the answer to a soul that is constantly troubled by guilt?

Notice again that it is the blood of Jesus that purges our conscience from dead works. The blood of Jesus is as alive today as it was when it

THE BLOOD OF JESUS TESTIFIES OF THE VICTORY OF THE CROSS AND DECLARES THAT SIN'S POWER HAS BEEN BROKEN.

flowed in the flesh of the Son of God. This blood cleanses and purges us from our sense of failure, inadequacy, and guilt. The blood testifies of the victory of the cross. The blood declares that sin's power has been broken. As we place our faith in

His sacrifice and His blood, we experience the sense that we are forgiven. It is as we place our confidence in His blood that we lose our sense of despair and guilt. A guilty conscience is replaced with a sense of forgiveness and mercy. Hiding from God is replaced by confidence in God. That is why we can, with boldness, enter God's presence with assurance and joy.

Look at what the writer of the Book of Hebrews says:

> Therefore, brethren, having boldness to enter the Holiest by the blood of Jesus…let us draw near with a true heart in full assurance of faith, having our hearts sprinkled from an evil conscience and our bodies washed with pure water.
>
> —HEBREWS 10:19, 22

It is not on our merit that we live, but on His merit. His precious blood constantly reminds us of this fact. Place your faith in that cleansing flow today. Accept His sacrifice for you. Celebrate His victory over your failures. Allow His blood to wash the guilt away from your conscience, releasing your soul to sing and declare His power and love!

9

Finding Your Worth
in His Love

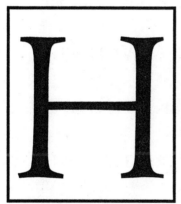

IS MIND REELED AS HE REMEMBERED the terror he felt when he first noticed the patch of white skin. It wasn't long before it was impossible to conceal the contagious disease beneath his clothing. He also remembered the most painful part of his sickness—the cool glances...the sneering looks of contempt.

It seemed to happen so fast....

Suddenly, the noise of the crowd jarred him back to the present as he saw himself surrounded by faces filled with hate. Faces of people that at one time he thought were his friends.

"Filthy sinner," the crowd angrily spat as they drove him several feet to the outskirts of town. With the taste of dust still in his mouth, the outcast collapsed to his hands and knees beneath the wave of painful emotions. The shame and disgrace were more unbearable than the knowledge of his impending death from this hellish condition.

Leprosy—God's death sentence for the sinner. God's judgment for the imperfect. At least that is what the religious leaders said.

It would be some time before the leper would dare to make his way back to town. But he did shortly after news of a man named Jesus began to filter through the colony—a different religious leader with a different message. Jesus didn't just preach, *He happened!* Because of Him, blind eyes opened; deaf ears were unstopped; it seemed no sickness or disease could survive His touch.

"If anyone can remove this curse, it is Jesus," the leper reasoned. The leper was fully aware of the possible consequences of his return to town—a slow but sure death by stoning. Still, stoning would be quick compared to watching his body waste away slowly. "I have nothing to lose," he concluded. His decision not only changed his

"IF HE IS INDEED WILLING, WHY WOULD HE BE?" WITHIN THE ANSWER TO THAT QUESTION IS THE ESSENCE OF THE GOSPEL.

life, but it helped to change mine as well.

In Mark 1:40–42 we read the rest of the story:

> Now a leper came to Him, imploring Him,
> kneeling down to Him and saying to Him, "If
> You are willing, You can make me clean."
> Then Jesus, moved with compassion, put out
> His hand and touched him, and said to him, "I
> am willing; be cleansed." As soon as He had
> spoken, immediately the leprosy left him, and
> he was cleansed.

In the past, I have heard wonderful sermons
from this passage. Most contrasted our belief in
God's ability while questioning His willingness to
demonstrate His ability on our behalf. I know that
God is all-powerful, and I can accept the fact that
He is willing. But as I thought about these
Scriptures I was struck with a more probing question: "If He is indeed willing, why would He be?"
Within the answer to that question I began to discover for the first time as a Christian the essence of
the gospel.

Most of us believe that the reason God sent His
Son was to save our souls from hell. At the risk of
sounding like a heretic, I want to say that is not
why God sent His Son to this earth. Now, anyone
who chooses to receive God's free gift of eternal
life, which is provided by Christ's death and resurrection, is redeemed from hell. And anyone who
rejects this wonderful gift will spend eternity apart
from God. But if we believe that is why Jesus died
on the cross, then we will have difficulty relating to
God for the rest of our Christian lives.

Mark 1:41 says that Jesus was "moved with compassion." *Compassion* refers to an emotion that

comes from the depths of a man. This was a violent passion, one that made it impossible for Jesus *not* to respond and reach out. Jesus couldn't help but reach out to this man. He didn't reach out because of *sympathy*—that is too distant. You and I can feel sympathetic toward someone and still not be involved. It wasn't because of *pity*—that is too condescending. *It was love that moved Jesus!* Love always demands action. In John 3:16 it says:

> For God so loved the world that He gave His only begotten Son, that whoever believes in Him should not perish but have everlasting life.

Normally we emphasize the last part of the verse: If you and I receive Jesus, we can avoid spending an eternity in hell. Even though this is true, we must keep in mind that the last part of the verse— the promise of eternal life—is only there because of the first part of the verse—"For God so loved the world."

Through the religion this leper had learned from the religious leaders of history, his sense of worth and value had been stripped from him. His hope had been crushed by the cruel hands of the controllers. When Jesus reached out and touched this leper, He loudly declared the leper's worth and value. It wasn't a worth that came from a sacrifice of religious duty. It didn't come by careful observance of self-imposed regulations. It came because Jesus chose to place His love upon the unlovable. By doing this, Jesus forever decreed value and significance over this leper's life. This act of compassion had nothing to do with the leper and everything to do with Jesus. There was nothing that the leper could do to manufacture this love that

Jesus had for him, nor could he do anything to min-imize it. It was unconditional. It was who Jesus was. It was love's nature.

All my life I had based my worth on what I did for God. I was convinced that when I failed in some way, my failure minimized God's love and acceptance of me. I had no real understanding that God's love for me was truly unconditional.

Consequently, it was through my service to Him that I attempted to gain His favor. And not only was it important to gain God's favor—I also desperately needed the acceptance of those around me. I con-stantly lived with this ledger in my mind, always hoping that at the end of the day my good deeds would outweigh my bad.

It seemed that the harder I tried to resist tempta-tion, the weaker I became. I never really experienced any peace—at least not for any length of time. I finally reached the point where I would collapse with exhaustion from attempting to live that day in the strength of my own will power. I opened my eyes each morning under the crushing weight of that familiar blanket of oppression, facing another day of trying to gain His love.

This philosophy of thinking on which I had built the castle of my life came crashing down that fateful Sunday night in November. Even as I held the pistol in my hand, I knew I had nothing left to offer God. But unlike the leper, my sickness, as well as the shame and hopelessness that followed, were self-inflicted. I had dug this horrible pit for myself through my own sin. My life had been ravaged with the disease of insecurity and pride. Every good thing that God had given me I had crushed beneath the heel of my own rebellion. I had sinned against God...I nearly destroyed my marriage...I lost the church...and I violated the trust of the people.

My life was a wasteland filled with the debris of broken promises and shattered dreams. A wasteland that I had created through my own self-centered choices. As I sat there surrounded by destruction, I had no place else to look but to the One whom I had resisted. I honestly did not know what His response would be. I knew what I deserved, but I was shocked by what I heard.

Let me first of all tell you what I didn't hear. I didn't hear a scathing lecture filled with "I told you sos." But I did hear God speak to me—I heard Him whisper these words:

"Mike, I have redeemed your life from destruction, and from the pit, and I have restored beauty and dignity." (See Psalm 103:3–4.)

"But God," I interrupted, "I know You see what I've done and the mess I've... "

He continued, "Mike, listen...I said I have redeemed your life from destruction.... "

Again I interrupted, "But God, how? More importantly...why?"

My heart slowly melted as He finished by saying, "By crowning your life with My lovingkindness and tender mercies. And that, Mike, has nothing to do with you and everything to do with Me!"

GOD'S LOVE BUILDS SECURITY

I came to the amazing realization that God loved me as much when I was swinging my legs from a stool in the local strip joint as He did at the moment of genuine repentance. By resting in His passion for me, I was delivered from the other passions that had enslaved me. In chapter five of this book I mentioned that insecurity is a doorway of deception. A revelation of God's love is the only way to shut the door of insecurity. Finding our security in His love establishes our hearts and releases His ability in the face of temptation. Paul writes:

> But God—so rich is He in His mercy! Because of and in order to satisfy the great and wonderful and intense love with which He loved us, even when we were dead (slain) by [our own] shortcomings and trespasses, He made us alive together in fellowship and in union with Christ.
>
> —EPHESIANS 2:4–5, AMP

The motive behind redemption is the startling fact that God was unwilling to do without us. His love was so intense that it had to be satisfied. Therefore, you and I became the object of His satisfaction! We are the object of His joy.

THE FUTILITY OF WORKS IN GAINING HIS ACCEPTANCE

Through discovering His love for me, I was able to escape the trap of trying to earn God's love and acceptance through good works. No longer did I find myself doing all the right things for all the wrong reasons, through pride placing my trust in what I could do, yet all the while never feeling that I had done enough.

In the tenth chapter of Mark, the Bible illustrates the futile trap of trying to earn God's favor. In this passage we see an interesting scenario taking place between Jesus, a rich young ruler, and the disciples.

One day as Jesus walked through the countryside, a young man approached Him and knelt before

Him, saying, "What shall I do that I may inherit eternal life?" (v. 17). This young man was rich, a ruler in his country, and he wanted to know how he could add to his wealth the one thing that up to this point in his life had eluded him—eternal life.

Notice the response of our Lord. "Why do you call Me good? No one is good but One, that is, God" (v. 18). Jesus, knowing the spirit in which this young man was approaching Him, rejects his flattery. As Jesus continues His conversation with this man, He lists the last five of what we commonly call the Ten Commandments. The young ruler responds that he has kept all of these commandments since his youth.

"Then Jesus, looking at him, loved him" and in essence said, "Then I want you to liquidate all of your assets and give them to someone who can't do anything for you—the poor. Then deny yourself, take up your cross, and follow Me" (v. 21).

The Bible records this about the wealthy young man: "He was sad at this word, and went away sorrowful, for he had great possessions" (v. 22).

But you and I know that those great possessions *really had him.* By being unwilling to part with his wealth, this ruler exposed that in which he had placed his trust: *He had more faith in the power that came with his riches than he was willing to put in Jesus.* The young ruler was enamored with Jesus' power, but he had no real interest in knowing the Savior.

Now this is where the story really gets interesting. Jesus spins on His heels and says to the disciples, "How hard it is for those who have riches to enter the kingdom of God!" (v. 23). The disciples were astonished at this saying. In other words, what Jesus said to them rolled them back about seven feet and really shook them up. Our Lord went on to clarify what He had said: "Children, how hard it is for those who trust in riches to enter the kingdom of God! It is easier for a camel to go through the eye of a needle than for a rich man to enter the kingdom of God" (vv. 24–25).

This didn't help the disciples much, and at this point they cried out in complete frustration saying, "My God, then who can be saved?"

Jesus replied, "With men it is impossible, but not with God; for with God all things are possible" (v. 27).

I must say that it was not hard for me to understand the response of the rich young ruler. After all, it was obvious that he was trying to buy his way into the kingdom. But for the longest time I could not understand the anxiety of the disciples. Especially later on in verse 28 when Peter asserts that they had left all to follow Jesus. Apparently the disciples did what the rich young ruler was unwilling to do. Yet, obviously what Jesus had said bothered them.

Like that of the rich young ruler, the disciples' response exposed that in which they placed their trust. Jesus told the rich young ruler, "Young man, you cannot *buy* your way into the kingdom." To the disciples Jesus had said, "My friends, you cannot *give* your way into the kingdom." The rich young ruler's faith was in what he *possessed*. The disciple's faith was in what they had *given away*. Jesus was saying that neither of these responses is enough to qualify a person for eternal life—or for *His acceptance*.

What would our response be if after we did our best, as perfectly as we could, giving it our all, Jesus turned and told us, "That's not enough!"? Well, if our confidence was in what we did, our response would probably be the same as the disciples· "If that isn't good enough, Jesus, then what is?"

The answer is…NOTHING.

The reason why I always had the sense that whatever I did was never enough was because *it wasn't enough*. It never would be enough. No matter what I did, it would not be sufficient.

As believers, we know that we need God. We know that without Him we have no hope of heaven or victory here on this earth. Even though we know that we need Him, each of us has an earthy bent toward self-sufficiency. Yes, I need God, but somehow through human effort I will be able to apprehend Him. As if God were some trophy I could win. So, through some good work, some extreme sacrifice, or some good deed, I am going to win the prize of God.

Remember the words of Jesus: "With men it is IMPOSSIBLE." There is nothing that we can do…give…or sacrifice that will ever be enough. It is not what *we do,* but what *He has done* that enables us to experience the life-changing power of His love. It is only when we are aware of our impotence and inability that we can truly place our faith in His ability, thus experiencing the power of the cross.

What is the purpose then of our good works? Simply this—what we do for Him needs to be a celebration of what He has already done. Our good works are not some service we render to Him, trying to earn something that He has already given to us. After all, God is not the one to be apprehended—we are. He is not the one to be conquered—we are.

The key to this whole passage in Mark is found in verse 21:

Jesus, looking at him, loved him.

If the young ruler could have seen the love in the eyes of Jesus, gladly would he have traded in his entire empire just to be with the Master. The acceptance, worth, and significance the young ruler tried to achieve through his wealth would have paled in the light of God's love. In the same way, if the disciples could have understood the love Jesus had for them, they would have realized that the acceptance they desired from Jesus was already theirs.

Unfortunately, many times those of us who should be the closest to Him are the ones who are the furthest from His presence.

GOD'S LOVE BRINGS GENUINE BROKENNESS

It is at this point that we experience the power of His ability, which transcends the weakness of our humanity. It is when I realize how bankrupt I am in the light of His majesty that I begin to experience the power of faith in His life-changing love. *Only* in our weakness do we experience His strength. This is what I call the *weakness vs. power principle.*

For example, the apostle Paul prayed three times for the thorn in his flesh to be removed. After the third request, Jesus revealed to Paul a key to experiencing His power:

> And He [Jesus] said to me, "My grace is sufficient for you, for My strength is made perfect in weakness."...Therefore I take pleasure in infirmities, in reproaches, in needs, in persecutions, in distresses, for Christ's sake. For when I am weak, then I am strong.
>
> —2 CORINTHIANS 12:9–10

Paul was not saying that he believed God was the author of his tribulations. But Paul did recognize the opportunity of being reminded of his inability to overcome these trials. Therefore, in recognition of his weakness, faith was ignited in the power of the cross, which released God's supernatural power in Paul's life. No wonder Paul said in Galatians 6:14, "God forbid that I should boast except in the cross of our Lord Jesus Christ, by whom the world has been crucified to me, and I to the world."

The ultimate example of this principle is in the ministry of our Lord. We read Paul's reference to the ministry of Jesus in 2 Corinthians 13:4:

> For though He was crucified in weakness, yet He lives by the power of God. For we also are weak in Him, but we shall live with Him by the power of God toward you.

To the natural eye and by the standard of human reasoning, the cross was foolishness. Here was God in the flesh. The same One who created the universe was now pierced and imprisoned on a wooden beam. As He walked on this earth, He walked in power. He raised the dead, healed the sick, and walked on water. But now, this same Christ is subject to the frail hands and wicked hearts of mere men. To those looking on, Calvary looked weak, powerless, and foolish. It represented the failed expression of another dreamer gone mad.

Yet, the cross was God's ultimate expression of love and wisdom. This unassuming plan was in the heart of God from the beginning. It was God's strategy for foiling Satan's scheme against heaven. It was imperative that Jesus, in His humanity, be crucified in weakness. It was through the weakness of Christ's flesh that the power of God's Spirit could raise Him to live forever. It is also, as we accept the weakness of our flesh, that we experience the power of His Spirit quickening our mortal lives!

This is what I mean by brokenness. The brokenness of God is not sickness, disease, poverty, and calamity brought on by God. None of this would require the supernatural work of the Holy Spirit. For God to perform these acts of cruelty on His children would be against His very nature.

Brokenness comes as a result of the Holy Spirit's revealing the intensity of our weakness to accomplish anything for God or to accomplish the much-needed work of God within our lives. When we reach this point, we are broken. It is at this time that we are overcome with God's beauty and with the majesty of His love. Being overcome with God's passion for us always results in faith toward God, thereby releasing His power to perform His work of deliverance, healing, restoration, and the establishing of our hearts.

DISCOVERING HIS PLEASURE

I heard about two men who broke into a large department store. What caught my attention was the fact that these two men did not steal anything. Instead they changed the price of everything. Values were exchanged. A two-hundred-dollar VCR was tagged with a seventy-dollar price tag, and a seventy-dollar vacuum was priced at two hundred dollars. What is even more amazing is the fact that it was nearly four hours into the business day before anyone noticed!

I think that this is a perfect description of what

has happened to our society. We place a tremendous value on entertainment and talent and very little value on character. We vote politicians into office, believing they will make our lives more comfortable regardless of the fact that we do not feel we can trust them.

Satan broke into God's store and began to switch the price tags on God's ultimate treasure—you. Then he tried to convince us to accept the cheap value he placed on our lives. Jesus came to this earth and exposed the thief—showing us our true value and challenging us to rip the tags off and live within our royalty. Your worth compelled your Creator to come in the likeness of flesh, give His life, take upon Himself His own wrath and indignation, shed His own blood, raise Himself from the dead, and conquer death—just to restore your relationship with Him. And He did this simply because He loves you! Think about that the next time Satan attempts to slap on you a bargain-basement price tag through temptation.

Paul said that the love of God *constrains* us (2 Cor. 5:14, KJV). Another way to say this is to say that the love of God *compels* us. His love can compel us to live lives of godliness and integrity. Understanding His love does not give us a license to live after our flesh, but rather it draws parameters in our lives.

For example, I no longer succumb to the temptation of pornography and immorality because I now know that I don't have to. I don't need to fill a void of rejection by trying to be empowered by sex. I am loved! I am accepted by God. He declares that my worth is greater than the price with which Satan may tag me. The power of God's love gives us the strength to believe, the desire to press on, the freedom to love, the courage to laugh in the face of adversity, and the faith to live holy.

Are you still wondering what is His pleasure? Well, the answer is, YOU ARE. Regardless of what you have felt in the past, *YOU HAVE WORTH!* Your life counts. You are significant. There is nothing you did to earn that, and there is nothing you can do to erase that fact. *God loves you!*

10

Renewing Your Mind Regarding Your Past

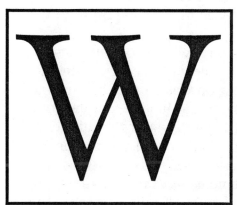

E HAVE THOROUGHLY discussed the subject of God's grace and our inability to earn His favor and love. What we do does not increase God's love for us, but the choices we make do make a difference in our lives here on earth. There are certain disciplines that we can embrace that will position us to receive the power of God's grace in our lives. In the remaining chapters I will be discussing the disciplines that enabled me to experience God's power and establish my identity in Christ.

Let's take a look at an earlier time in my life. I

had only been a Christian for two months, and I was not sure what to do with my life. Consequently, I decided to take some classes at the local community college. I signed up for a class studying the different religions of the world. I assumed that we would be spending most of our time on the subject of Christianity. I was wrong. I soon discovered that the professor was enamored with the eastern religions.

During one particular class, the instructor decided that we would sit in a circle together and practice the art of eastern meditation. I was admittedly uncomfortable as we all began to hum in unison. After some time, the instructor asked if any of us were feeling anything. I wanted to say, "Yeah, I am feeling something. I'm feeling like this is a big waste of time." That was my first exposure to the art of meditation.

Consequently, when I saw the word *meditation* in the Scriptures, I immediately recalled the event that took place in my religion class. I certainly had no desire to sit on the floor and hum before the Lord. Gradually, I started to understand the difference between eastern meditation and meditation on God's Word. With eastern religions as well as with the New Age movement, *meditation* is the art of emptying one's mind from all other thoughts and perspectives. (I'm not sure how much art is involved in that. I can remember plenty of times in life feeling pretty empty-headed.) At any rate, once a person has emptied his or her mind of all other thoughts, that person is able to receive spiritual guidance from their seers (demons).

I discovered that biblical meditation is the exact opposite of that which my instructors practiced. The word *meditation* actually means "to mutter to oneself." It also means "to muse, to consider, to think upon." I began to see that the way I was to meditate on the Word of God was to say it aloud. As I say God's Word aloud, I am forcing my mind to think about what I am saying. Biblical meditation is not the act of *emptying one's mind,* but rather *filling it with God's Word.*

MEDITATION ON GOD'S WORD RENEWS OUR MINDS

In Romans 12:2 we read, "And do not be conformed to this world, but be transformed by the renewing of your mind, that you may prove what is that good and acceptable and perfect will of God." This scripture indicates that the result of renewing our minds is that we experience a transformation in our lives. It is only through meditation on God's Word that we experience the renewing of our minds.

Still, there are misconceptions many Christians have regarding meditation that hinder the effectiveness of the Scriptures in their lives. For example, the act of just reading the Bible, though important, does not necessarily result in the renewing of our minds. Another popular misconception is that "confessing" God's Word equates automatically to meditation of God's Word. Confession of the Word of God does aid us in meditation. But I know people who quote Scripture all the time, yet their lives reflect very little of God's nature and power.

As we look closer at what the Scriptures say about mediation on God's Word, we begin to discover how it is accomplished.

But his delight is in the law of the LORD,
　And in His law he meditates day and night.
He shall be like a tree
　Planted by the rivers of water,
　That brings forth its fruit in its season,
　Whose leaf shall not whither;
And whatever he does shall prosper.
　　　　　　　　　　　　—PSALM 1:2–3

Notice what the scripture says about the man or woman who meditates on the Word of God. The psalmist says that person's life will be like a tree whose roots drive down so deep, tap into a river so full of life, that the tree of his or her life will always produce fruit and never whither. Whatever he puts his hand to will prosper. How is this accomplished? By meditating in God's Word *day and night.*

The Book of Joshua also speaks of meditating day and night:

> This Book of the Law shall not depart from your mouth, but you shall meditate in it day and night, that you may observe to do according to all that is written in it. For then you will make your way prosperous, and then you will have good success.
> 　　　　　　　　　　　　—JOSHUA 1:8

At first this seems impossible. It is kind of like 1 Thessalonians 5:17, which says, "Pray without ceasing." These are pretty intimidating scriptures, especially if you are a mother with small children or a wife and mother who works outside of the home. You may be tempted to throw your hands up in despair saying, "If it takes meditating on the Word day and night and praying without ceasing to renew my mind, I might as well give up!"

Before you despair completely, let me ask you a question: Have you ever worried without ceasing? Have you ever been full of anxiety day and night? I am sure that we can all honestly say that we know what it is like to worry without ceasing. Well, here is the good news. The same part of your soul that worries is the part that prays or meditates. In other words, since you have the capacity to worry without ceasing, you also have the capacity to pray and meditate day and night.

Meditation is not memorization. It is not thinking of each specific word in the Scriptures. *Meditation* is first of all recognizing the picture that the Scriptures paint for us. It may be a passage that brings us a picture of peace. Or a picture of healing for a sick body. Maybe it is a picture of provision. Meditation is carrying that picture of life around on the inside of us. It is exciting that our souls were created by God with the ability to carry a picture of victory around day and night. We certainly know what it's like to be overwhelmed with fear day and night. In the same way, our heart and mind can be saturated with the life of God's Word *without ceasing*. Even while we are asleep, our soul is able to be bathed with God's life-giving Word.

THE PRINCIPLE OF SEEING AND DOING

As we meditate on the Word of God, we attack and tear down the strongholds in our thought life. This is important because it is our thoughts that determine our actions. Your body or your life can never go in a direction that your thoughts have not previously gone.

113

God told Joshua that he was to meditate on His Word day and night "that you may observe to do according to all that is written in it." The principle is that we do what we see in our minds. The mind has two basic functions: memory and imagination. We are created by God to perform what we first see in our minds. Every action is first proceeded by a thought picture. For example, adultery does not come upon a man or woman like a seizure. The thoughts and fantasies of adultery are played over in one's mind long before the act of adultery takes place. I first started thinking about adultery through pornography. Then I began to see myself doing the same things that I observed on videos. It was only after a time of envisioning myself committing these terrible acts that I followed through with actions.

As we meditate on God's Word, we are allowing the Word to paint a picture for us of strength, purity, and victory. The process of exchanging these pictures is the process of "renewing" our minds. In fact, we really don't see with our eyes— we see with our minds. Our lives will rise and fall dependent upon the pictures we carry around on the inside.

When Joshua meditated on God's promises, he began to see himself performing and experiencing those promises, consequently making them a reality with his actions.

PULLING DOWN STRONGHOLDS AND CASTING DOWN IMAGINATIONS

When we understand the definition of a *stronghold*, then this principle of seeing and then doing makes even more sense. Most people think of a stronghold as some outside demonic force pressing in on them. But a stronghold actually comes from within and not from without.

In 2 Corinthians we read:

> For the weapons of our warfare are not carnal but mighty in God for pulling down strongholds, casting down arguments and every high thing that exalts itself against the knowledge of God, bringing every thought into captivity to the obedience of Christ.
>
> —2 CORINTHIANS 10:4–5

The actual definition of a stronghold is "arguments and reasonings, demonically inspired, that someone uses to fortify their opinions against their opponent." Strongholds exist between our ears. They come about as a result of the process of reasoning that Satan has convinced us to embrace. Strongholds are opinions and perceptions about which we feel strongly. Even though these thoughts seem right to us, they can be incorrect, unhealthy, and destructive.

A STRONGHOLD IS A SYSTEM OF THOUGHT EMPOWERED BY EMOTIONS.

To further understand what effect strongholds have on our lives, we need to take a look at the words *high thing*. These two words in English are actually one word in the Greek, which is *hupsoma*. Some of the words involved in the definition of this word are "barrier, rampart, or ceiling." In other words, Satan attempts to get us to embrace a process of reasoning, attitudes, and opinions that places ceilings on our lives spiritually.

Therefore, a *stronghold* can be any "destructive system of thinking." In my case, I had been controlled by a stronghold of sexual fantasies and desires, as well as strongholds of insecurity and fear.

In other cases, a stronghold may be an intense struggle with drugs, alcohol, violence, depression, a lust for power, or any other addictive thinking that preoccupies our minds to the point of being obsessive.

Even though these perceptions may be destructive to our lives, we continue to hold fast to them. Because they have become so much a part of our makeup and behavior, it takes a supernatural work of the Holy Spirit through the Word of God to expose these thoughts as incorrect. In fact, it is only the Word of God with the work of the Holy Spirit that has the power to expose these well-dressed lies.

THE POWER OF GOD'S WORD

Second Corinthians 10:4 says, "The weapons of our warfare are not carnal but mighty in God for pulling down strongholds." What are the weapons that God has given us? There are several, including the Word of God, the blood of Jesus, the name of Jesus, and the intercession of the believers. When we mix faith in with these weapons, we begin to experience the power of His grace.

The one weapon that I want to focus upon is the *Word of God.* You will understand why when we see how we cast down imaginations. God's Word is the only thing that the Holy Spirit can use to destroy destructive reasonings. God's Word is more than black words on white paper. It is supernatural.

> It is the Spirit who gives life; the flesh profits nothing. The words that I speak to you are spirit, and they are life.
>
> —JOHN 6:63

> All Scripture is given by inspiration of God [God breathed], and is profitable for doctrine, for reproof, for correction, for instruction in righteousness.
>
> —2 TIMOTHY 3:16

Scripture is the standard or rule by which we are able to judge whether what we are believing is correct, regardless of how strongly we may feel about it. His Word never changes—it is always the same. Our opinions may change, and we may deal with different perceptions in life, but God's Word endures forever.

When we pick up the Bible, we need to remember that it is *the book with God in it*. It is not just black words on white paper. Actually, it is more than a book that tells us about God—it is a supernatural work. You cannot separate God from His Word. The same attributes that apply to God apply to His Word. Since we know that God is faithful, we know His Word is faithful. If God is all truth, and it is impossible for Him to lie, then we know that the Scriptures are truth, and we can trust them with our lives. Stop seeing the Bible as just a book written about God. Begin to look at the Scriptures as an expression of the heart of the Father. The Scriptures are a living, breathing testament of God's will for your life.

Most Christians look at the Scriptures simply as a manual for living. Even though that is partly true, if that is the only revelation you have of the Bible, then your time in the Word will be dry and lifeless. In John 1:1 we catch a glimpse of the true nature of the Scriptures:

> In the beginning was the Word, and the Word was with God, and the Word was God.

The fourteenth verse of John 1 tells us:

> And the Word became flesh and dwelt among us...

Let me share more Scripture passages that dramatically show the nature of the Word.

> Now I saw heaven opened, and behold, a white horse. And He who sat on him was called Faithful and True, and in righteousness He judges and makes war. His eyes were like a flame of fire, and on His head were many crowns. He had a name written that no one knew except Himself. He was clothed with a robe dipped in blood, and His name is called The Word of God.
> —REVELATION 19:11–13

You see, the Word is like its Author—eternal... powerful...victorious...living! The Word is the out-breathing of God. It is God speaking to you today. It speaks of winning, victory, joy, and surrender. His Word speaks of prosperity, healing, and victory over sin! The Word of God has the supernatural ability to change your life from the inside out! Ask the Holy Spirit to breathe the truth of His Word into your heart today. Receive His power and life.

God's Word has the power to help us discern the source of our faith, and it enables us to discern if what we are thinking is from God.

> For the word of God is living and powerful, and sharper than any two-edged sword, piercing even to the division of soul and spirit, and of joints and marrow, and is a discerner of the thoughts and intents of the heart.
> —HEBREWS 4:12

As we consistently expose our thoughts and feelings to God's Word, it is the light of His Word that exposes our true motives behind our feelings and subsequent decisions. As we continually expose our minds to the Word of God, we will see our thoughts and imaginations for what they really are.

The Bible is the primary source by which we are able to examine our emotions to see if our feelings line up with the truth. Hebrews 5:14 tells us, "But solid food belongs to those who are of full age [mature], that is, those who by reason of use have their senses [emotions] exercised to discern both good and evil." It is as we continue to put the Word of God into practice that we begin to "crack the whip" of His Word over our emotions, training them to recognize between right and wrong, enabling our will to respond to the truth.

MY PERSONAL JOURNEY

This process is lifelong. Because we live on this planet and in this "earth suite," we will be subject to temptation. Renewing our minds is a lifestyle. For me, it was the only way that I was going to be able to conquer the controlling impulses of my thoughts and imaginations. There are different methods we can use to meditate on God's Word. I want to share in detail the exact method that worked for me. Again, you may find another method more effective. It is not so much *how* we do this; it is just important that we *do it!*

Shortly after moving to Chicago, I sat down in my kitchen and wrote down several scriptures on three-by-five-inch index cards. Even though I initially wrote down twenty or more scriptures, I found myself concentrating on seven to ten scriptures. These scriptures had to do with the subjects of the power of God's Word, His righteousness for me, and the power of His love toward me.

I would get up every morning, take a shower, get dressed, and go into the living room. Then I would begin to pray, thanking God for His grace and mercy. I would ask the Holy Spirit to help me as I prayed and meditated on the Word of God. I would worship Jesus and His majesty. Then, I would begin to read aloud one verse at a time. I would take my time with each verse, saying it several different ways, personalizing each truth.

For example, one scripture on which I meditated was Colossians 1:13:

> He has delivered us from the power of darkness and conveyed us into the kingdom of the Son of His love.

I might then say, "Father, I thank You that You have delivered *me* from darkness and have jammed me, by Your power, into Your kingdom of love. I am now controlled by Your love and not by Satan's kingdom! Satan's kingdom has no power over me!"

Then I would pray as I looked at that verse. I would continue praying until in my spirit I sensed His peace bear witness to this truth. Many times, though, because my mind was so undisciplined, it would disagree with me. As soon as I would say the verse, I would have the thought that I wasn't really delivered from Satan's power. But I continued this process every day, meditating on five to seven scriptures in this manner.

One day, after about fifteen months, something startling happened. I got up and went through my usual regimen; not only did I sense His peace in my spirit, but in my mind I heard this forceful statement, "Yes, you are delivered from Satan's power—you are controlled by the power of God's kingdom!" I had reached the point where God's Word wasn't just a truth to me—it was becoming *the* truth. The words upon which I had been meditating all this time were becoming more real to me than the past—or anything else that was happening in my life. The reality of the challenges I was facing financially, in my marriage, and in other areas were still there. I recognized these issues. But I began to see that these things were subject to the authority of God's Word and what He had to say about me. For the first time in my Christian life, my mind was bowing its knee to the authority of God's Word.

The tormenting thoughts of the past with which I had struggled for years began to loosen their hold over me. With a revelation of God's love and grace, His Word was finally becoming more real to me than anything else that had happened to me. As a result of accepting God's love for me, the difficulty I had with really loving my wife disappeared. I experienced greater peace and a greater commitment to my family and my God. His Word works! It is real, and it is filled with supernatural power.

Have you found yourself struggling with familiar sin or tormenting memories of yesterday? Do you battle thoughts of lust, depression, anger, or defeat? Have there been times in your relationship with God when it seems that you have run up against a barrier? Have you reached an impasse in your marriage, career, or relationships? The answer is found in God's Word. Have you allowed the Word of God to examine the attitudes and opinions in your life?

Take a few moments to take inventory of your thoughts. You may be dealing with a mind-set that is contrary to God's Word. Are you willing to make the necessary adjustments? If so, then God's Word is able to do within you what you could never do by the strength of your own will. Embrace the discipline of meditating on His Word. Discover the miracle of the power in the Word of God.

11

Prayer—Discovering Freedom in the Place of Intimacy

N THURSDAY MORNING, APRIL 11, 1996, Jessica Dubroff, her father, and her flight instructor were preparing to take off from the airport in Cheyenne, Wyoming. At the ripe age of seven, Jessica was on her way to becoming the youngest pilot ever to successfully complete a continental flight.

As I sat in my hotel room, I watched the slow-motion video of Jessica, with a mobile phone to her ear, jogging toward the single-engine Cessna in the pouring rain and sleet. They wanted to take off as soon as possible in an attempt to beat a storm front that was beginning to blanket the northwest.

I listened to the interviews as Jessica expressed

her love for flying and breaking records. I listened to her father talk about the importance of allowing children to make their own decisions, even if they were only seven years old.

Within minutes after takeoff, the plane stalled four hundred feet in the air. Seconds later, it slammed into the end of a neighborhood driveway. In a panoply of twisted metal and shattered glass lay the bodies of little seven-year-old Jessica, her father, and her flight instructor. They were killed instantly.

We can learn many lessons from this tragedy. The one that stands out in my mind the most is this: *Knowledge without experience is deadly!* Why? Because it builds a false sense of security. It is one thing to know mentally the mechanics of flying. It is another to have experienced the dynamics of being a pilot. Jessica was beginning to gain the one, but she will never have the chance to experience the other.

The same principle applies spiritually. Knowing *about* God is not the same thing as really *knowing* God. If we reduce God to a doctrine or a chapter and verse, we may completely miss the life-changing power of His presence. For example, the Greeks' understanding of knowledge was simply an accumulation of facts. It was a mental ascent. From that line of thought came a religion known as *Gnosticism,* which basically was a worship of knowledge. The Greeks assumed that the more one knew *about* something, the more spiritually advanced one became. It did not matter if your life was unaffected by what you knew—it only mattered that you knew it.

In contrast, the Jewish definition of knowledge went beyond a mere mental understanding. In the Jewish mind, to *know something* was to have *personally experienced it.* Paul wrote in Philippians 3:10: "That I

124

may know Him and the power of His resurrection, and the fellowship of His sufferings, being conformed to His death." Paul's goal was not just to acquire more facts about Jesus, His life, and His ministry. Paul was referring to a revelation of the person of Jesus that came as a result of experiencing His presence personally. Out of that experience Paul was confident that he would be conformed to Christ's death; therefore he would live in the power of Christ's resurrection. Paul is describing a personal knowledge that resulted in a transformation of his life.

If we are not careful, we can trust more in what we know *about* Christ than we do in our personal experience of His presence. Head knowledge is never enough to make it through life and finish our course strong. Head knowledge can do nothing to change us. We must be willing to commit ourselves to practicing His presence.

Jesus confronted the religious leaders on this very issue:

> You search the Scriptures, for in them you think you have eternal life; and these are they which testify of Me. But you are not willing to come to Me that you may have life.
>
> —JOHN 5:39–40

Jesus was saying that the Pharisees trusted merely in their ability to interpret the Scriptures. Their confidence lay in the power of their intellect to understand the issues of life found in the Word. Coming to Jesus for eternal life requires an attitude of humility, which admits that we have no capacity in ourselves to receive life.

The Bible is not an end in itself. The purpose of

the Scriptures is to point us to the person of Jesus! Therefore, in order to receive life from the Scriptures, we must approach the Word in the same way by which it originally came to us. As the Holy Spirit breathed on men's hearts, the Scriptures were penned. Therefore, in turn we must allow the Spirit to once again breathe on the pages of our Bibles.

I must be honest with you. If it were not for the illumination of the Spirit, I would much rather do a lot of other things more than reading my Bible. It is the Spirit who brings life to the Word, branding its truth upon our souls.

In the place of prayer we begin to know *Him*— not just more *about* Him. It is through the communion of the Holy Spirit that God's Word is quickened to us. It is imperative that we allow the Spirit to breathe life upon the Word we hear and read. If not, our hearts can become hardened to the very truths that have the ability to change us. Consequently, our life with Him becomes dry, mechanical, and stoic, lacking any real joy and power.

PRAYER ENABLES US TO TAP INTO THE POWER OF HIS WISDOM

Jesus talks about the importance of instruction from the Holy Spirit through prayer, speaking of prayer's ability to guard our hearts against deception. In Luke 11:1 we read:

> Now it came to pass, as He was praying in a certain place, when He ceased, that one of His disciples said to Him, "Lord, teach us to pray, as John also taught his disciples."

I am sure that by this time in their lives the disciples had prayed a lot of prayers. Here is another time when the disciples have silently observed Jesus' divine exchange with the Father. Something about the way Jesus prayed made the disciples feel that they really didn't know how to pray. So, after Jesus was finished, they tugged on His cloak and said, "Please teach us how to do that." Recorded in the next few verses is Jesus' secret to effective prayer.

Jesus first gives them an outline of prayer, one which we have traditionally referred to as the Lord's Prayer (Luke 11:2–4). Then Jesus teaches His disciples how to break through with power in prayer (vv. 5–13). In this parable Jesus teaches the principle of breaking friendship with the world in order to pull down bread from heaven to feed a dying humanity. In other words, Jesus is teaching on the power of intercessory prayer.

After He teaches His disciples the power of prayer, an incident takes place where Jesus drives a demon out of a man, loosing his tongue and enabling him once again to speak. This incident results in a confrontation between Jesus and the religious leaders. The religious leaders attempt to minimize Jesus' influence on the hearts of the people in the synagogue by accusing Him of casting out demons by the power of Satan.

When Jesus is aware of this accusation, He asks the Pharisees a question. The answer to His question will determine if Jesus really is of the devil.

> If I cast out demons by Beelzebub, by whom do your sons cast them out? Therefore they will be your judges.
>
> —LUKE 11:19

Jesus is saying, "If I exercise power over demons by the power of Satan himself, how do your disciples exercise power over demons?"

The Pharisees didn't respond. They couldn't—because neither they or their disciples ever cast out demons. Why? Because they had no power over Satan's kingdom.

Then Jesus continues by saying:

> But if I cast out demons with the finger of God, surely the kingdom of God has come upon you.
>
> —VERSE 20

In other words, Jesus was saying, "If I cast out demons, be assured that it is by God's power. Therefore, if I cast out demons and you don't, then I must be the one that is of God, and you must be the ones that are of the devil."

In verses 21 and 22, Jesus says:

> When a strong man, fully armed, guards his own palace, his goods are in peace. But when a stronger than he comes upon him and overcomes him, he takes from him all his armor in which he trusted, and divides his spoils.

Let me paraphrase what Jesus is saying: "If you are going to get so upset over Me casting out some low-level demon, you should know that you haven't seen anything yet. Satan has existed on this earth without rival. He has been the strong man on this earth. No one has been a worthy opponent—at least not until now. A stronger than the strong man is here. Casting out this demon is nothing compared to what I am going to do. There will be a time when I will walk right into the master bedroom of the strong man himself and overtake him and strip from him his armor. I will accomplish a victory so complete that Satan will never get over it. To the victor goes the spoils, and I will take those spoils and give them to whomever I wish, and there is nothing in hell you can do to stop Me!"

Jesus continues His teaching by saying that when the kingdom of God invades a man's life, that man can live free of the dominion of Satan.

> When an unclean spirit goes out of a man, he goes through dry places, seeking rest; and finding none, he says, "I will return to my house from which I came." And when he comes, he finds it swept and put in order. Then he goes and takes with him seven other spirits more wicked than himself, and they enter and dwell there; and the last state of that man is worst than the first.
>
> —LUKE 11:24–26

The Book of Matthew says that when the unclean spirit returns he finds the man "garnished" (Matt. 12:44, KJV). The word *garnished* means "to be elaborately furnished." In other words, this man is equipped with all the weapons necessary to exercise authority over Satan's kingdom regarding his life. He possesses the name of Jesus and the Word of God. The nature of life dwells within him. Because of this, there is no way that this unclean spirit by force can take over this man's life again. If the unclean spirit is to accomplish his work of destruction, it is going to require deception. If he cannot storm through the front door to plunder this man's house, then he must, through deception, talk this man out of his possessions. Consequently, Jesus says that this unclean spirit appeals to seven other spirits more powerful than he to accomplish this work of deception. The Scripture continues by saying that this man succumbs to the deceptions of these spirits, and Jesus says, "The last state of that man is worse than the first" (v. 45).

This parable serves as a warning about the dangers of living by our own perceptions. The apostle Paul warned:

> Now the Spirit expressly says that in latter times some will depart from the faith, giving heed to deceiving spirits and doctrines of demons.
>
> —1 Timothy 4:1

We desperately need the wisdom of God. Either we live by our own wisdom, or we live by the wisdom that comes from above.

> But we speak the wisdom of God in a mystery, the hidden wisdom which God ordained before the ages for our glory, which none of the rulers of this age knew; for had they known, they would not have crucified the Lord of glory.
>
> —1 Corinthians 2:7–8

It was the wisdom of God that placed Jesus on the cross, thereby redeeming mankind back to God and establishing victory over principalities and powers. It is God's wisdom alone that serves as a safeguard against Satan's deceptions. Who applies the wisdom of God to our hearts? It is the Holy Spirit—our teacher and counselor. Jesus called Him *the Spirit of truth.*

PRAYER RELEASES OUR TEACHER

Prayer is the discipline that releases the Holy Spirit to teach us. It is through this teaching process that we really come to know Him. As we pray over the Scriptures, the Holy Spirit brings us instruction. This enables us to *experience* personally the reality of the Word Himself. If we do not welcome this process, then our relationship with Jesus becomes nothing more than cerebral.

Notice what Jesus said about the Holy Spirit in John 14:26: "...He will teach you all things, and bring to your remembrance all things that I said to you." In John 16:13 we read, "However, when He, the Spirit of truth, has come, He will guide you into all truth."

First John 2:27 tells us, "But the anointing which you have received from Him abides in you, and you do not need that anyone teach you; but as the same anointing teaches you concerning all things, and is true, and is not a lie, and just as it taught you, you will abide in Him."

IT IS POSSIBLE TO QUOTE SCRIPTURE AND STILL BE UNAFFECTED BY IT. PRAYER SATURATES THE SOUL WITH TRUTH.

John is not saying that we no longer need pastors and spiritual leaders to teach us. What the apostle John is saying is that if we do not expect the Spirit to reveal personally the truths that we hear preached, then what we hear will never change our lives. The same applies to the time we spend reading and meditating upon the Scriptures.

Within the process of the Holy Spirit's teaching us we discover the difference between what I call *insight* and *revelation*. As we read the Scriptures, the Holy Spirit will often illuminate a specific verse or passage. I am sure that you have experienced this. A particular verse seems to reach out and grab you. Many times we will see a truth within a particular verse that we have never noticed before. As a result, we can't wait for the next opportunity to amaze our Christian friends with our new "revelation."

Actually, what we have is simply a divinely inspired insight. Insight is good, but it is only the beginning. *Revelation* results when our lives have been conformed to that divinely inspired insight. In other words, when that insight so impacts me that it actually becomes a part of who I am, only then can I say that I have experienced a new revelation. *Only through prayer do these truths have an opportunity to become revelation to us through the instruction of the Holy Spirit. Through prayer the Word of God is quickened, bringing the understanding we need concerning our lives.*

Allow me to further illustrate this point. In Mark chapter 4, Jesus shares with us the parable of the sower. The focus of this parable is not upon the seed that is being sown, which is the Word of God. The focus is upon the condition of the soil, which is our hearts. It was the condition of the soil that determined the amount of fruit that was produced. Through this parable Jesus teaches us that the condition of our hearts will determine the fruit of His Word that is produced out of our lives. Jesus went

132

on to say that the heart that is healthy will produce thirty, sixty, even a hundredfold of the fruit of God's Spirit in their lives.

Then, in the next verse, Jesus shares how we can avoid the pitfalls that befell those in whose lives the fruit of the Word was choked out.

> Is a lamp brought to be put under a basket or under a bed? Is it not to be set on a lampstand? For there is nothing hidden which will not be revealed, nor has anything been kept secret but that it should come to light.
>
> —MARK 4:21–22

The purpose of the lamp is to illuminate. The lamp provides the necessary light to govern our direction. The lamp lights the room, enabling us to go from the front door to the back without tripping over the coffee table. Consequently, it serves no purpose to take the lamp and hide it under the bed. The light from the lamp will only work if we put the lamp in its proper place—on the lampstand. Then the lamp lights the whole room, and we can see clearly.

The lamp is the Holy Spirit. The lampstand is the Word of God. Through the work of the Spirit the Word comes alive in our hearts and minds. Through this process the hidden things of our hearts are revealed. What hidden things are these? The attitudes and mind-sets seated deep within our souls, which have the ability to choke out the fruit of God's Word in our lives. But if we allow the Spirit to breathe the life of God's Word into our hearts, then those hidden attitudes of the soul are revealed and can be purged from our hearts.

The work of the Spirit, brought about by prayer over God's Word, exposes things in our lives that cause us to sabotage our own success. The Spirit enables us to recognize why we continue to be drawn into one abusive relationship after another...why we continue to be passed over for the big promotion...why we are never able to find victory over our finances. We see this principle at work when Jesus drove out the money lenders from the temple.

> So they came to Jerusalem. Then Jesus went into the temple and began to drive out those who bought and sold in the temple, and overturned the tables of the money changers and the seats of those who sold doves. And He would not allow anyone to carry wares through the temple. Then He taught, saying to them, "Is it not written, 'My house shall be called a house of prayer for all nations'? But you have made it a 'den of thieves.'"
>
> —MARK 11:15–17

Jesus said that the temple was meant to be a house of prayer...a house of divine exchange...exchange between God and His people. Yet, the money changers and religious leaders had prostituted the hunger of the people. As a result, the temple had become a den of thieves. A place that robbed the people of their right to a divine exchange between them and God. We have "money changers" in the temple of our hearts. Thieves that rob us of our intimacy with the Father. Thieves of unforgiveness, bitterness, pride, and ambition. When we pray, we are releasing the Holy Spirit to fashion His whip and turn over the tables of these enemies. Once these areas of our soul are transformed, then we are in a position to produce thirty, sixty, even a hundredfold of His nature on our lives.

PRAYER IS A POSTURE OF DEPENDENCE

One morning I read Mark 1:35, which says, "Now in the morning, having risen a long while before daylight, He went out and departed to a solitary place; and there He prayed." After I read this verse, the Spirit said, "Mike, this was the secret of Jesus' power in life and ministry." Now, I do not want to imply that if we want to experience power in life we must pray in the early morning hours. Rather, what struck me was the *habit* of prayer that defined Jesus' life. Along with this fact was the dependence upon the Father that was demonstrated in Jesus' life of prayer.

When Jesus prayed, it was more than just an example of how we too should pray. While Jesus was clothed in humanity, He was subject to temptation just as we are. He was very aware of the weaknesses within the flesh. Therefore, He knew the importance of assuming a posture of utter dependence upon the Father's wisdom and ability. Daily, Jesus reestablished this attitude of dependence within His place of prayer.

As Jesus prayed, He received instruction from His Father. In John 5:19 Jesus Himself said, "The Son can do nothing of Himself, but what He sees the Father do." It was in the place of prayer that Jesus heard the words from the Father that He was to teach the disciples. It was through prayer that our Savior's vision was propelled by the light of eternity. Ultimately, it was in prayer that the Son of God battled and overcame the desire for self-preservation, sacrificing Himself for all humanity.

We too can experience power over self. We can live in a spirit of dependence and surrender to the will of the Father. Our lives can be guided by God's eternal perspective. But these things will only be accomplished in the same place in which they were accomplished in the life of Jesus—the place of prayer.

UNDERSTANDING THE SEASONS OF PRAYER

People struggle with many perceptions about the subject of prayer. Many believe that one must be locked up in solitude for hours each day to experience God's power and pleasure.

OUR PRESENT SEASON OF LIFE WILL OFTEN DICTATE THE TIME AND METHOD OF PRAYING.

For example, when my sister became a Christian, she was single and had more time for extended prayer. Now she is married and has four young children. Their home is never boring, to say the least. If she spent hours a day locked away in prayer, she would be neglecting her other God-given responsibilities. She is now in a different season of life. As a result, this requires a different season of prayer.

I am sure that she is able to take advantage of time here and there in private prayer. But she also has the opportunity to practice His presence throughout her daily duties. Prayer is simply communion with God through the work of the Holy Spirit. Consequently, my sister can maintain an attitude of prayer in the midst of her daily chores and responsibilities.

First Thessalonians 5:17 tells us to "pray without ceasing." This verse has brought condemnation to many of us. If prayer required me to lock myself away in a room, then I could never obey this Scripture, at least not without sacrificing other areas of my life. But let me ask you, "Have you ever worried without ceasing?" Well, the part of you that worries is the same part of you that prays.

No matter what we are involved in, we can direct our thoughts and hearts toward God in communion, not only speaking to Him, but being open to receive from Him as well. There are times when God desires us to separate ourselves for the purpose of prayer. But it is important to understand that those times should not violate other areas of our lives upon which God has placed value.

THE SAFEGUARDS WITHIN INTIMACY

Our intimacy with Jesus guards our lives from acts of sin. For example, it is impossible for a man to commit adultery while maintaining a life of emotional intimacy with his wife. That man must take steps away from intimacy to make room for another woman. That is why I say that adultery never overtakes a man like a seizure. Not only must he imagine adultery first in his mind, he must also reduce emotional intimacy with his wife as well. The same principle applies with our relationship with God. We must take systematic steps away from intimacy with Him in order to make room for sin in our lives.

I want to encourage you to accept His invitation to intimacy. As you meditate on His Word, allow the Spirit to breathe His Word into every chamber of your soul. He's waiting. Even if it has been a while since you've stepped into the secret place, know this: He's not angry—He just misses you.

12

Strike the Iron and
Let the Sparks Fly

I N THE SECOND CHAPTER WE OPENED WITH A picture of Peter struggling with the shame of his failure after he denied his knowledge of Jesus. In his despair, Peter had gone back to his original occupation of fishing. It may be speculation on my part, but I believe that James and John were there with Peter to encourage him. I can almost hear these two friends reminding Peter that Jesus prophesied this denial would happen. But they also reminded Peter that Jesus said he would be restored and would minister life to others. Whatever was happening in that boat, the point is this—Peter was not alone. He had two friends that were with him when the "chips" were down.

It was during this difficult time that the disciples

relied on each other the most. It is a wonderful example of the power of relationships. *Peter might not have recovered from the failure of his past as quickly without the encouragement of James and John.* It is true that our friends can determine, to a degree, our destiny.

THE POWER OF A FRIEND

Show me a man's companions, and I'll show you what he's made of. One of the most accurate spiritual barometers of someone's life is the people with whom he chooses to keep company. At the very least, we know this is true when it comes to our children. Parents have concerns about the company our children choose. We know the reality of the scripture in 1 Corinthians 15:33: "Bad company corrupts good morals" (NAS). We have seen it either in our own children or in the children of our friends and neighbors. It is so easy to spot the negative influence of other children. Their behavior smacks of adolescent immaturity.

Unfortunately, the negative influence that is so easily detectable in children is sometimes harder to discern in adulthood. I have found that many times as adults we make three major mistakes when it comes to relationships:

1. We give little thought to the power of relationships.
2. We have difficulty in recognizing negative relationships.
3. We do not know how to develop godly relationships.

I want to look at what the Scriptures say about

the value of healthy relationships, as well as the dynamics involved in establishing and maintaining godly relationships.

IMPORTANCE OF GODLY RELATIONSHIPS

A wonderful example of the importance of godly relationships is found in Paul's second letter to Timothy. Timothy was facing a defining moment in his life and ministry. The decisions that Timothy would make in the next few months would greatly affect his future. Notice what Paul says:

> Flee also youthful lusts; but pursue righteous-ness, faith, love, peace with those who call on the Lord out of a pure heart.
> —2 TIMOTHY 2:22

Often as I read this verse previously, I missed the significance of two words: "…with those." In other words, Paul was telling Timothy that as he pursued the things that bring life—righteousness, faith, love, peace—he was not to pursue them *alone*. Timothy needed to surround himself with those who were also in pursuit of God. The apostle Paul knew that within these relationships an environment would be created allowing the dynamic of God's grace to flow through Timothy's life.

We can identify another important principle: Godly relationships must be pursued. Very rarely, if ever, do they happen out of convenience. The only kind of friendships that happen out of convenience are the ones we usually don't need in our lives. It is our responsibility to pursue healthy friendships. Many times people take the position of a wall flower, waiting for someone to initiate a relationship with them. If you want godly friends, then you must make it happen.

> A man who has friends must himself be friendly.
>
> —PROVERBS 18:24

In Proverbs 27:17 we read, "As iron sharpens iron, so a man sharpens the countenance of his friend." According to this verse there is a dynamic involved in godly relationships—as we relate to one another as Christians, exchanging the flowing out of the life of God from within, each of us will enhance our relationship with God. Those who are surrendered to His lordship offer a portion of God's Spirit and wisdom to others that we could never gain on our own.

IT IS NECESSARY TO ESTABLISH HEALTHY LIFE-GIVING RELATIONSHIPS WITH OTHER BELIEVERS.

One of the most life-changing discoveries that I have made is that Jesus and I alone are not enough to escape the pitfalls of life. I know that this may sound like heresy to some, but according to Scripture we are a part of a body and were never meant to function independently of ourselves.

> For as the body is one and has many members,
> but all the members of that one body, being
> many, are one body, so also is Christ. For by
> one Spirit we were all baptized into one
> body—whether Jews or Greeks, whether slaves
> or free—and have all been made to drink into
> one Spirit. For in fact the body is not one
> member but many.
>
> —1 Corinthians 12:12–14

The body is not *one* member, but *many!* In order
for me to experience the full benefit of the grace of
God in my life, it is necessary for me to establish
healthy life-giving relationships with other believers.

RECOGNIZING HEALTHY RELATIONSHIPS

All throughout God's Word we are commanded to
abandon unhealthy relationships and develop
godly relationships. Whenever God wants to bless
you, He will send someone in your life as the
vehicle of blessing. Whenever Satan wants to
destroy your life, he will send someone in your life
as the vehicle of destruction. The people around us
either increase us or decrease us. There is no neu-
tral zone in relationships.

Several times the apostle Paul admonishes us to
avoid destructive friendships. Look at what he says
in 2 Thessalonians 3:14–15:

> And if anyone does not obey our word in this
> epistle, note that person and do not keep com-
> pany with him, that he may be ashamed. Yet
> do not count him as an enemy, but admonish
> him as a brother.

Here we see the balance between not exposing ourselves to a contentious attitude in someone and at the same time attempting to reach out to them with godly instruction. The reason that we are instructed to avoid them is not because we see ourselves as better than they are, but because we understand human nature and recognize that we can't afford to be exposed to a contentious atmosphere consistently.

Here are some simple guidelines to help you recognize unhealthy relationships:

- They have a general angry attitude toward life.
- They constantly gossip about others.
- They remind you of your past.
- They demand inordinate loyalty at the expense of other relationships.

Healthy relationships:

- challenge and build your faith in God through the way they live their own lives.
- cause you to remember God's faithfulness and love for you.
- testify of God's love.
- challenge you to a life of godliness and simplicity.
- recognize your potential and desire to see you reach that potential.

TRANSPARENCY

Developing godly relationships requires living a life of transparency. In James 5 we read, "Confess your faults one to another, and pray one for another, that ye may be healed" (v. 16, KJV). First, I want to qualify the meaning of this scripture. The apostle James is not advocating that we confess our faults to just anyone who is available. Those to whom we confess should be mature in the Lord, able to keep confidences, and spiritually qualified to help.

What we see in this verse is the sacredness of relationships. I believe that the dynamic of God's healing power is released not only because of the faith expressed in prayer, but also because of the faith demonstrated *in God* by being transparent.

One of the most important elements to experiencing the total benefit of godly relationships is that of transparency. For example, if someone is struggling with familiar sins, a life of transparency is an important step to finding freedom and victory. It is important to understand that any stronghold of sin is built on the foundation of deception. Therefore, secrecy empowers temptation and familiar sin. A common trap of Satan's is to convince us that there is no one with whom we can be honest.

Many times this is because we have been hurt in the past. As a result, we hesitate in becoming vulnerable. We fear that someone will again take advantage of us in our time of weakness. Unfortunately, this becomes a deadly paradox. While we are holding others at arm's length, we continue to make room for deception in our lives. Once we make the decision to become honest and shed light on our weaknesses, we immediately begin to weaken the grip of the particular stronghold.

I remember when I decided that I would take the risk of being transparent. This was a tremendously liberating time in my life. I began to experience great freedom in my conscience when I decided that my relationship with God was more important than what people thought about me. That's when I decided to live honestly before my wife, Bonnie, and others.

This may be difficult at first. We may have the habit of "covering" ourselves by projecting the image we desire people to have of us. Or we may feel that we have no one with whom we can afford to be honest. In light of the importance that God places on a life of transparency, I believe that even if we feel there is NO ONE in whom we can confide, if we will ask God to show us someone, we will discover He has provided each of us with someone we can trust.

ACCOUNTABILITY

Not only is it necessary to have healthy life-giving friendships, but being transparent involves establishing relationships of accountability as well. Before I continue, I want to address a popular misconception regarding the subject of accountability.

Accountability is not *servitude*. The definition for *servitude* in the American Heritage Dictionary is "a state of subjection to an owner or master; lack of personal freedom as to act as one chooses." There is only One who is our Master and owner. He is the One who purchased us with His own blood. He is the only One who has the right to demand a relationship of such extreme measures. If we enter a relationship of servitude with another person, we are giving them a place that belongs only to God. Therefore, being accountable in a relationship does not require the relinquishing of your will over to that person.

Accountability is intended to help strengthen your relationship *with God*. It is not for the purpose of developing co-dependent relationships at the *expense* of our relationship with God. There are plenty of people who would be more than willing to run your life for you. These folks are well-versed and skillful in weaving certain scriptures in an attempt to place inordinate demands on others. They usually veil these demands under the guise of "spiritual authority," exacting obedience that they define as being "loyal" to the man of God. They may even tell you that their counsel is the only advice to which you should listen—and if their narrowly viewed advice is not heeded, then one is in rebellion and open to the destruction of Satan.

The problem is that this concept completely ignores Proverbs 11:14, which states that "in the *multitude* of counselors there is safety" (emphasis added). Whatever spiritual strength you may feel you develop through such a relationship of extreme, isolated authority, it is really an illusion. It is not the empowerment of the Spirit at work in your life—it is the result of a soul tie. Your faith and confidence is in the acceptance and approval of another man—it is not in your trust in Jesus. Consequently if that relationship ever sours, then you may find yourself drowning in a sea of self-doubt, fear, and confusion.

A healthy relationship of accountability is one that directs you toward a more intimate relationship with Jesus. Such a relationship will challenge you to take responsibility for your own relationship with God, as well as for your own choices in life.

Accountability is a choice to expose yourself to the wisdom and counsel of others who are spiritually mature. When we understand accountability,

147

we will willingly ask for godly counsel. And we will assume our own responsibility for listening and choosing what is right.

I want to encourage you to begin to develop relationships of accountability and transparency. Ask the Holy Spirit to show you the people He has brought into your life. People that not only can be a vehicle of His blessing, but also those whom you can bless. Discover the power of God that is available in godly relationships. Go ahead, strike that iron and let the sparks fly!

The Subtle Power
of Consistency

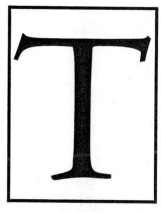

HERE IS A DEAR PASTOR FRIEND OF mine whom I always enjoy being around. He has been the pastor of the same church for almost as long as I have been alive. When I am with him I can sense the spiritual force of consistency. He has had thousands of opportunities to quit; he has faced adversity on many fronts. Yet, for every opportunity he had to quit, he made a choice to continue in God's purpose for his life. The strength of his life is not just in continuing to pastor the same church. But within his perseverance, he made choices to guard his integrity.

As a result, when I am around him there is a

depth of character that I find contagious. It's the battle scars of life accompanied with character that cause consistency to be a spiritual force. Consistency is not glamorous, but it is an essential key to our spiritual health and strength.

In 2 Timothy 2:22 we read, "Flee also youthful lusts; but pursue righteousness, faith, love, and peace with those who call on the name of the Lord out of a pure heart." Notice the first part of the verse—"Flee also youthful lusts." Most of the time we interpret this scripture within a sexual connotation. Yet, another way to interpret "flee also youthful lusts" would be "flee the passions of youth" or "flee the sins of immaturity." We normally think of lust within a sexual connotation. Actually, lust is any inordinate passion that becomes a driving force in our lives crippling us from being able to be consistent.

What are the sins of immaturity? I believe that according to the Scriptures they are *discontentment* and *impatience*. As long as these two characteristics go unchecked, we can never live a life of consistency.

DISCONTENTMENT

Discontentment springs from a dissatisfaction with the present circumstances of our lives. There is a thin line between spiritual hunger and discontentment. If we don't have God's wisdom, we are unable to discern between the two. As a result, we begin to remove our trust from God's Word, placing it in earthly sources to accomplish much needed change. A good definition of *discontentment* is "the belief that God's Word is no longer enough." It was through discontentment that Satan was able to become the god of this world. How else do you tempt two people who are living in paradise? Satan could not tempt them with the cares of this world— they didn't have any physical needs. They couldn't be tempted with adultery—there were no other people on the earth.

Satan had to convince Adam and Eve that God was "holding out on them." They had to be convinced that there was something they should have that God was not allowing them to possess. They became discontented. As a result, they were able to justify disobeying God.

When the promises of God regarding our future, as well as our present, seem insufficient in our own eyes, we begin to employ other means to secure the future that we feel we deserve. *When we do this, it always involves our integrity being compromised.* Discontentment is certainly a symptom of "youthful lusts." Notice what the apostle Paul says in Philippians 4:11: "Not that I speak in regard to need, for I have learned in whatever state I am, to be content." In 1 Timothy 6:6 we read, "Now godliness with contentment is great gain."

IMPATIENCE

The second enemy of consistency is *impatience.* *Impatience* is simply refusing to trust God with your future. Impatience comes when we see time as an enemy instead of as a friend. As long as we see time as an enemy, we will never be able to embrace time and allow patience to have her perfect work.

For example, there may be areas of our lives that we do not like. Many times, these are things that have been a part of who we are for years—they are

151

not going to change overnight. Change requires *time*. Time is one element that God has reserved within His sovereignty.

Let me explain. No one knows the time or hour that Jesus will return—not even Jesus Himself. This great event has been reserved by God within His sovereignty. With matters of time (how long...?, when...?), God requires that we trust Him. God only gives us clues—"soon," "shortly," or "quickly." He rarely gives us the exact hour or moment.

The Bible says that as we allow patience to have her perfect work, we become mature and lack nothing (James 1:4). If I am impatient I cannot be consistent. I will always be looking for shortcuts in life and will never follow through with anything. Patience allows me to expose those areas of weakness in my life. Jesus said, "By your patience possess your souls" (Luke 21:19). As I submit to the force of patience, I am expressing my trust in God's faithfulness. I am also releasing the dynamic of consistency.

CONSISTENCY: A RETURN TO THE BASICS

Consistency is a powerful and necessary dynamic in our lives. Consistency provides a place where we recognize and learn the lessons from the past. As we faithfully administer the principles of God's Word, we begin to identify where in the past we strayed from the fundamentals of the faith. Understanding this is imperative in order not to repeat the past again. I have learned from personal experience that whenever Satan shipwrecks our faith, it is never over some deep revelation. It is always in the area of the fundamentals.

Allow me to further illustrate this point. Michael Jordan once discussed why after a few years many NBA players experience difficulty in their performance on the court.

He said that throughout their careers many of them rely on their size and strength. But as these players are getting older and slower, the younger players are getting faster and stronger. As a result, the veterans are not able to perform as well. The reason? Michael Jordan explained that early in their careers they neglected to give their attention to the *basics*. The *fundamentals*, if you will. It is a fact that many things change over time. Yet the one thing that doesn't change is the fundamentals; the only thing that does change concerning the basics is our attention to them.[1]

NEGLECTING THE BASICS OF OUR FAITH ALLOWS SATAN TO INFILTRATE OUR LIVES WITH DECEPTION AND EVEN DESTRUCTION.

The same is true for Christianity. If we neglect the basics of the faith (prayer, meditation on the Scriptures, godly relationships, faithfulness, and obedience, for example), Satan is able to infiltrate our lives with deception and even destruction.

Consistency is a celebration of the basics! It keeps the reality of Jesus alive in our hearts and gives the basics freedom of expression in our lives. The Word of God becomes relevant and active in our homes. For example, because consistency requires patience, our souls are trained to submit to God's wisdom. It is through consistency that we are able to experience the wisdom of God. As we saw in chapter eleven, it is through prayer that we *hear* and *see* the wisdom of God. Yet, it is only through consistency that we *experience* the power of God's wisdom. There is a enormous difference between the two. One allows His life to flow through us; the other is just empty knowledge.

Once we see His wisdom, we must allow it to have expression in the daily, decision-making process of life. If not, then what we have seen and heard in prayer just becomes merely an intellectual assent. This is why many Christians receive wonderful insight from the Scriptures, but they are not able to experience the power of those same principles in their daily lives. As we consistently apply our lives to His truths, especially in the face of adversity, His character is able to be fashioned and formed in us. That is when these insights translate into personal disciplines, transforming our lives into His image.

THE DYNAMIC OF FAITHFULNESS

When we talk about consistency we must talk about faithfulness. In 1 Corinthians 4:1–2 we read:

> Let a man so consider us, as servants of Christ and stewards of the mysteries of God. Moreover it is required in stewards that one be found faithful.

154

In Matthew 25:14–29 we read about the parable of the talents. This lengthy parable carries several vital principles concerning faithfulness. First of all, each of the three servants had the same opportunity, even though they weren't given the same amount of money. They each had the same opportunity to faithfully steward the master's wealth according to their own unique ability and not the ability of the other servants. The way the master measured their faithfulness was by increase, yet he didn't expect the man with the one talent to produce the same amount as the servant with ten talents. He just expected his servants to produce.

When we take a look at the servant who received the one talent, we see some perceptions that paralyzed his ability to be faithful. Notice what Matthew 25:25 says: "And I was afraid, and went and hid your talent in the ground. Look, there you have what is yours." The servant said he was "afraid." Fear clouded his perspective of life. First of all, I believe this servant struggled with a fear of failure. The fear of trying, only to experience defeat. Consequently, the servant would rather take his chances with the master than face the issues within his own soul that sentenced him to a life of mediocrity. *The fear of defeat must be conquered in order for our lives to be a reflection of faithfulness.*

Many are aware of the difficulties that surrounded Abraham Lincoln's life, yet his life is a perfect example of one who didn't fear failure. In 1831 Lincoln failed in a business venture. In 1832 he decided to run for the legislature and was defeated. In 1833 Lincoln tried his hand in business again, only to suffer another defeat. In 1836, one year after his sweetheart died, Lincoln suffered a nervous breakdown. In 1838 he was defeated as speaker for the house. In 1840 he was defeated for elector as well as losing the race for Congress in 1843. He was finally elected to Congress in 1846, only to be defeated for the same office in 1848. Lincoln ran for the Senate in 1858, losing the election. Finally, in 1860 Abraham Lincoln was elected president of the United States.

Booker T. Washington once said, "Success can be measured not so much by the position one has achieved in life, but by the obstacles one has overcome while trying to succeed." Abraham Lincoln's life certainly illustrates this truth. And when the future of our country was at risk because of civil war, it was the wisdom of President Lincoln, a man familiar with hardship, that brought healing to our nation.

Lincoln was not alone. Many great men of history refused to give up, allowing faithfulness and consistency to bring eventual victory. George Frideric Handel had lost his health, was paralyzed on one side, and was ruined financially. It was during this time that he wrote the immortal "Hallelujah Chorus." When Thomas Edison invented the light bulb, he was almost totally deaf. John Milton was nearly blind when he wrote *Paradise Lost*. Beethoven continued to write symphonies after losing his hearing.

In Proverbs 24:16 we read, "For a righteous man may fall seven times and rise again, but the wicked shall fall by calamity." God is not nearly as concerned about punishing us as He is about perfecting us. The truth of the matter is that many times consistency is demonstrated by getting up after we have fallen. Once we have, we place our faith in His mercy, and by His Spirit we determine to do it right the next time.

Another important principle is that fear caused the servant to have a distorted view of the master. Fear caused this servant to automatically assume that the master was an unjust man. This fear resulted in the servant treating with contempt the thing of value that the master had entrusted to him. He took the master's money and buried it in the ground. Fear always clouds our ability to recognize those things that are of real worth. Fear causes us to treat with contempt those things that are of real value—relationships, responsibilities, marriages, families, or careers. Fear blinds us with self-absorption. We see others as the reason for our failures or difficulties, embracing a victim's mentality toward life.

Is there something of value in your life that fear has caused you to bury in the mud of shame? Are there gifts, talents, and abilities that God has deposited in you that you've buried in your own personal darkness? Maybe within a friendship, fear of rejection has caused you to be blinded to the value of the relationship. Perhaps it's a marriage that's gone from bad to worse and the fear of a marital fatality has caused you to want to "throw in the towel." What is the thing of value that you still have? Your will. Your ability to choose and to believe.

Victor Frankle, after he had been captured and imprisoned by the Nazis, was stripped of everything he owned—even his family. Yet, as he lay in his cell, it dawned on him there was one thing that the enemy could never take from him. There was one thing of immense value that no man could seize from him—his power of choice. Victor Frankle still had the ability to choose. To choose to forgive and not allow himself to be the victim of hatred. To choose compassion and allow God's love to guard his heart from bitterness. You have the same choice today. There is a sacredness to the human will that lifts us beyond the common and brings dignity and nobility to an ordinary life.

CONSISTENCY REQUIRES ENDURANCE

Many times, life has a way of crashing in around us. Sometimes we feel as if we can handle it, trying to reason our way through that dark tunnel of trial, but at other times it seems as if we will never see the "light of day." Businesses sinking into the hole of a dying economy...marriages void of passion...medical reports silently screaming "cancer"...bills towering higher than the checkbook...we wonder what to do next. Futility and despair sink in. We face the stone walls of life while the voice of the world whispers cruelly, "Hopeless!"

A life of consistency is crucial during times like this. In 2 Timothy, God's Word gives us hope and wisdom for those times "when life seems too tough." Allow me to give you a little background into Timothy's situation.

Timothy was living in a time when persecution against the Christians was at its worst. The smell of blood was in the air in Ephesus where Timothy was pastoring. The spirits of fear and self-preservation were running rampant. Even many of Timothy's trusted leaders had departed from the faith in order to save their own lives. Timothy himself was wrestling with the emotions of panic.

Yet, in the midst of all this, Paul tells Timothy to "endure hardship as a good soldier of Jesus Christ" (2 Tim. 2:3). In essence Paul was saying, "Don't wish for things to get easier; decide that you are going to get tougher!"

This philosophy flies in the face of modern American Christianity. Many times we feel that the easier it is, the more God is involved. If it is easy and painless, it must be God. As a result, we find ourselves looking for the path of least resistance, often compromising principle along the way.

The fact of the matter is that Jesus never promised us a life void of trial. In fact, God's Word indicates the opposite:

> Yes, and all who desire to live godly in Christ Jesus will suffer persecution.
>
> —2 TIMOTHY 3:12

> No one should be shaken by these afflictions; for you yourselves know that we are appointed to this.
>
> —1 THESSALONIANS 3:3

Jesus Himself said in John 16:33, "In this world you will have tribulation; but be of good cheer. I have overcome the world." He says, "Take courage; I have overcome the very thing that troubles you."

WE MUST REMEMBER WHO OUR GENERAL IS

In 2 Timothy 2:4 we read, "No one engaged in warfare entangles himself with the affairs of this life, that he may please him who enlisted him as a soldier." Paul is admonishing Timothy: "When you don't think that you can make it—consider who your General is." He reminds Timothy, "Remember who enlisted you."

Down through history, for every great man, you can find another who is his counterpart. In the field

159

of philosophy you can parallel Socrates with Plato or match Aristotle with Cicero. In the field of poetry there are those who say that Alfred Lord Tennyson's poem "Crossing the Bar" is as great a work as Henry Longfellow's "Psalm of Life." Others might say that John Masefield—who cried, "I must go down to the seas again, to the lonely sea and the sky, And all I ask is a tall ship and a star to steer her by"—was as powerful as Robert Burns, the brilliant Scott poet.

In the field of literature John Milton, the blind poet who penned such literary classics as *Paradise Lost* and *Paradise Regained,* was as prolific as William Shakespeare, the immortal bard of the Avon. In the area of oratory Horace Greeley—who said, "Go west, young man; go west"—can be matched with William Jennings Bryan, whose campaign slogan was "You shall not crucify mankind upon a cross of gold." In the field of statesmanship we can match Abraham Lincoln with George Washington. We can parallel Thomas Jefferson with Henry Clay or Robert E. Lee with John Adams.

In the field of preaching John Knox, who prayed, "Give me Scotland or I die," can be matched with Martin Luther, who nailed his theses on the door of the enemy. We have men like Dwight Moody compared with George Whitefield, John Wesley compared to John Calvin.

Yet when it comes to Christ, He has no comparison. In Matthew 12:42 we read:

> The queen of the South will rise up in judgment with this generation and condemn it, for she came from the ends of the earth to hear the wisdom of Solomon; and indeed a greater than Solomon is here.

Jesus has no counterpart. He has no parallel. He stands alone—supreme, unique, and august. The greatest phenomena that ever appeared on the horizon of mankind. All similes and all metaphors merely skirt the edges of His matchless glory. This sacred Christ is the One in whom all victories and sufferings unite. His name blossoms on the pages of history like a million gardens combining all their beauty into one grand bouquet. His name sings down the corridors of time like a thousand choirs, visible and invisible, pouring their voices into one grand anthem. His presence is a spice that has perfumed every continent and people group. His every bone is divine sculpture. His every heartbeat is divine pulsation, and His every nerve is divine handwriting.

He is the Ancient of Days. He is the image of the invisible God, the Firstborn over all creation. He is the One who rides on a white horse wearing a vesture dipped in blood inscribed "King of kings and Lord of lords." His hair is like snow and His eyes like flames of fire. Out of His mouth goes a two-edged sword, and His voice is the sound of many waters. (See Revelation 19:11–16.)

Paul wrote:

> For by Him all things were created that are in heaven and that are on earth, visible and invisible, whether thrones or dominions or principalities or powers. All things were created through Him and for Him. And He is before all things, and in Him all things consist.
>
> —COLOSSIANS 1:16–17

He inhabits eternity. God's faithfulness is established in His eternal quality. Because He is eternal,

He transcends the imitations of time. He is always here; He lives in the dynamic of the now. And yet, there is another important quality to the eternal. Eternity is not subject to the laws of increase or decrease. Consequently, our Lord Jesus Christ is not subject to increase or decrease. He is unchanging and constant. Even when we are not faithful, He is. He doesn't change, and His Word still carries His life and love. It is important for us to understand that He builds on that which is eternal, not on that which is temporal. What He has done in our hearts and for us is eternal. Our past, our sins, and our failures—these are temporal. When we live in the shame of the past, we are placing more value on our failures than on the power of His blood. We are celebrating our sin over His victory. We must learn to celebrate what He celebrates. And He celebrates us! With all of our weaknesses, imperfections, and failures we are still the object of His joy.

It is His colors we wear, His image we bear, and His weapons that we wield. Do you really think that if we choose to believe, choose to endure, and choose to fight, there is any chance we will lose? There is not any more chance of us losing than in *our General* losing. We can afford to be consistent. It is in our consistency that His ability is released. It doesn't take a genius. It may require that we get up, though. And it will require that we simply put one foot in front of the other until we cross the finish line. The good news is that we can make it because He has already guaranteed us the victory!

I challenge you to embrace the discipline of consistency. Resist the temptation to live by the urgent. Choose to see time as your friend, allowing contentment to be the mark of your life. It is through consistency that we continue to distance ourselves from the past. It is through the power of consistency that we are able to walk through the consequences of the past.

I realized that in my life I was not going to be able to pull off some grand act of holiness and undo the consequences of my past actions. it would be "line upon line" that I would survive the past. Consistency and patience *always* release the dynamic of God, enabling us to walk step by step in victory!

Notes

Chapter 5
The Exaltation of Self

1. A. W. Tozer, *The Knowledge of the Holy* (San Francisco: Harper, 1992), n.p.

Chapter 6
Living in Duplicity

1. Paul Harvey, *Paul Harvey's For What It's Worth* (New York: Bantam Books, 1991), 141.

2. Dr. Robert McQuilken's letter is quoted from Richard Exley's book, *The Making of a Man* (Tulsa, OK: Honor Books, 1993), n.p.

Chapter 13
The Subtle Power of Consistency

1. Michael Jordan, *I Can't Accept Not Trying* (San Francisco: Harper, 1994)

If you would like more information about Mike and Bonnie Fehlauer or their ministry, please contact:

FOUNDATION MINISTRIES
P. O. Box 3099
Colorado Springs, CO 80934
Phone: 719.635.2064

You can experience more of *God's grace* & *love!*

*I*f you would like free information on how you can know God more deeply and experience His grace, love and power more fully in your life, simply write or e-mail us. We'll be delighted to send you information that will be a blessing to you.

To check out other titles from **Creation House** that will impact your life, be sure to visit your local Christian bookstore, or call this toll-free number:

1-800-599-5750

For free information from Creation House:

CREATION HOUSE
600 Rinehart Rd.
Lake Mary, FL 32746
www.creationhouse.com